Sandals in the Dust

M. E. Rosson

Jesus did many other things as well. If every one of them were written down, I suppose that even the whole world would not have room for the books that would be written. John 21:25

ISBN: 1-4392-0678-3

EAN13: 9781439206782

To order additional copies, please contact us.
Booksurge Publishing
www.booksurge.com

1-866-308-6235

orders@booksurge.com

Also by M. E. Rosson:
All the Books of the Bible-NT Edition-1st Timothy/2nd Timothy/Titus
All the Books of the Bible-Volume One-Genesis
All the Books of the Bible-Volume Two-Exodus
All the Books of the Bible-Volume Three-Leviticus
All the Books of the Bible-Volume Four-Numbers
All the Books of the Bible-Volume Five-Deuteronomy
Abraham and the Middle East Today
Sandals in the Dust (Paperback)1st Edition
Sandals in the Dust-Lives of the Apostles(Hardcover)

Available on Amazon.com in Paperback and Kindle editions

Acknowledgements

It has been almost 5 years since I Published the first edition of this book and almost 40 years since I first began to research this material. The response has been so overwhelming that I was determined write a second edition with even more information. The reason there is more information is that I have continued to research and study and have found more stories about these 12 men who changed the world. I want to ensure the reader that these stories are not meant to be an addition to your Bibles in any way, but to give us an historical look at the Apostles. I have been asked by many to give them my sources, and to them I say, read. Read all of Bede, Josephus, Pliny, The Golden Legend, Anti-Nicene Fathers and many others. These stories are all there to be found. They are the forgotten history of those who have laid the foundation for all of us.

To Anne and Cecil Who started me on the right path.

Table of Contents

Prologue

How can I tell the story of people I have come to know so well without first setting the backdrop of their homes and their families? There were many people who followed Jesus those three years and it should not be surprising that many of them knew Him well long before Jesus said, "Follow Me." While the Bible tells us much of Peter and Paul's journeys in the book of Acts, almost nothing is know of the other ten. Also there were women who played a large role in the spread of Christianity and virtually nothing has been written of them as well. In the following chapters we will deal with the lives, ministries and deaths of the original Eleven, The theories as to why Judas betrayed his Master, Three Sisters named Mary, Matthias and even Barsabas or Joseph the Just.

First you must understand that while Matthew, Thomas and Matthias were not from Galilee, the other nine were and knew Jesus quite well. Let me share a small part of a little known genealogy:

There was a Woman known as Anna and she had a sister named Ismeria Anna was widowed twice and married three times, Ismeria only married once. Anna had a daughter named Mary with each Husband who in turn married and had the sons listed below. Ismeria was the maternal grandmother of John the Baptist.

1)Anna/Joachim----2)Anna/Cleophas----3)Anna/Salome-----Ismeria

Mary/Holy Spirit	Mary/Alpheus	Mary/Zebedee	Elizabeth
Jesus Our Lord	James	James	John the Baptizer
	Simon	John	
	Jude		
	Barsabas(Not Chosen to replace Judas Iscariot)		

As you can see from the chart above, five of the chosen Apostles were First Cousins of Jesus and according to many writings, James the son of Alpheus looked almost like a twin of Jesus except for his eyes. These men all lived in and around Galilee and their families were able to band together for support when they were away following Jesus.

Many may view the fact that Joseph returned to Galilee after his exile in Egypt as a mystery, but like many of us would do, he was just returning home to be with family.

Phillip and Nathaniel who were also brothers were from a family of herdsman near Cana. James, Simon and Jude Alpheus were Carpenters just like Joseph and our Lord Himself. While Joseph and later even Jesus and His half-brothers were thought to be furniture makers, the Alpheus family brothers, including Barsabas, were said to be builders of houses. Of course most people know of the two sets of brothers, who were Fisherman, namely Simon Peter and Andrew and the famous Sons of Thunder, James and John. Both Matthew and Thomas were Levite and were Twin Brothers. Thomas was trained as a priest while Matthew was a Tax Collector, which was a Roman task given to the Levite Priests. Do you see a pattern forming in Jesus' plan! All of the original twelve were sets of brothers except for Judas Iscariot and later, Matthias.

The two years when Joseph stayed in Bethlehem, he befriended a young Shepherd Boy named Matthias. Legend tells us that Judas Iscariot was trained in the temple beside Thomas. The Alpheus Brothers built the house that was next to Mary and Martha of Bethany and that Joseph and even Jesus made the furniture for both of these homes. This was where Matthew and Thomas grew up. How could they sit in a chair or at a table made by the Master and not be affected.

The miracle that family and friends would follow Jesus has greatly affected my view of the Gospels. Most of us are somewhat comfortable sharing our faith in Church or maybe to a stranger. The truth of it is neither my brother, cousins or friends would follow me anywhere, except maybe to a free lunch! What does this say about the example that Jesus set for them to follow long before His Ministry began. They knew Him well and yet they still followed Him.

Again let us look at Mary mother of Jesus, Mary mother of the Alpheus Brothers and Mary mother of James and John Zebedee. We have Three Sisters who share the same Mother, Anna, but different fathers. Can you imagine the impact on your family if your half-sister Mary was suddenly pregnant, says something about an Angel and that she was still a Virgin? Worse she is engaged and she readily admits that the baby does not belong to Joseph, her husband to be. What a scandal! Then her betrothed husband to be says he will marry her anyway, they go to Bethlehem to pay some taxes. Two years later Roman Soldiers sent from Herod are looking for Joseph and Mary and their son. Stories of babies being murdered by the Romans come to Cana and the worst is feared. Rumor comes to the family that through some unusual gifts from Kings coming from the east that Joseph, Mary and the two-year old child are on their way to Egypt. Years go by, nothing is heard. Then about nine years later when Herod has died and the two-year-old is almost twelve Mary, Joseph and her children return to Galilee.

What a homecoming that must have been for Mary, to be re-united with her sisters. They must have all decided to go up to Jerusalem together at that time and we know the story well from the gospel of Luke. From the start the two Aunt Mary's must have been astonished at Jesus' behavior when he stayed behind and again when Mary allowed this run-away to go unpunished. He must be about His Father's business? What business could Joseph have had in Jerusalem? He had been out the country for almost 10 years! Who could Joseph have business with in Jerusalem? Well at least the boy seemed to be intelligent, or that's what the Priests at the Temple had said.

I have tried to allow you to see the childhood story of Jesus through the very human eyes of family. Being even a half-sister to Mary mother of Jesus would have been difficult at best. Of course we know the whole story from beginning to end and that makes it easier to believe than if this same situation was happening to us. I have always had a strong belief in God, but if my Sister told me she was pregnant and that she was still a Virgin, in today's enlightened age of science, I would have trouble believing her. Even Joseph was going to put Mary away quietly until God intervened with a heavenly visitation. Yet with all of these rumors and stories going around, when Jesus began his ministry, the three sisters were there much of the time. It is likely that all of the cousins were there as well. They were there when Jesus turned water into wine. They were there when Jesus was baptized by His cousin John and the voice spoke "You are my beloved son, in you I am very pleased."

Mary the mother of James and John Zebedee passed away weeks before Jesus was crucified. Her last request was that Jesus would put her two sons at His right and left hand when He established His Kingdom. When John stood there with his two aunts you remember Jesus last request of him. John had recently lost his mother and Jesus said "Woman behold your Son, Son behold thy Mother." Jesus was telling a mother that she had a new son and a cousin that his Aunt was to become his Mother. All of Jesus' family followed and believed in spite of the rumors. Again what does this say about our Savior? What kind of man can live a life that puts to rest all doubt and rumor? Only a life that is perfect and a Man that was and is the Son of God can inspire this type of devotion from family and friends, let alone others.

The chapters that will follow will chronicle each of these lives as completely as possible. We will start with the twelve and go on to others less spoken of in the scriptures but equally important to the spread of Christianity. Their sandals walked the dusty trails to Jerusalem, Israel, and to the uttermost parts of the World.

Many people today have imagined the kind of Men and Women that followed Jesus. Unfortunately in today's society of modern education we have seen to many Renaissance paintings depicting our Lord and his 12 in an almost feminine way. Nothing could be farther from the truth. These were men who lived and worked outside. They were rough, tough fisherman, carpenters, and herdsman. Even being a tax collector and a priest was not a task for the faint of heart in those days with the Romans watching your every move.

The early 20th century Poet Ezra Pound puts it far better than I in his poem, *"The Ballad of the Goodly Fere"* and here it is supposedly from the mouth of Simon Ben Alpheus, after the crucifixion.

Simon Ben Alpheus, Apostle, speaking after the Crucifixion.
Fere=Mate, Companion.

Ha' we lost the goodliest fere o' all
For the priests and the gallows tree?
Aye lover he was of brawny men,
O' ships and the open sea.

When they came wi' a host to take Our Man

His smile was good to see,

"First let these go!" quo' our Goodly Fere,

"Or I'll see ye damned," says he.

Aye he sent us out through the crossed high spears

And the scorn of his laugh rang free,

"Why took ye not me when I walked about

Alone in the town?" says he.

Oh we drank his "Hale" in the good red wine

When we last made company,

No capon priest was the Goodly Fere

But a man o' men was he.

I ha' seen him drive a hundred men

Wi' a bundle o' cords swung free,

That they took the high and holy house

For their pawn and treasury.

They'll no' get him a' in a book I think

Though they write it cunningly;

No mouse of the scrolls was the Goodly Fere

But aye loved the open sea.

If they think they ha' snared our Goodly Fere
They are fools to the last degree.
"I'll go to the feast," quo' our Goodly Fere,
"Though I go to the gallows tree."

"Ye ha' seen me heal the lame and blind,
And wake the dead," says he,
"Ye shall see one thing to master all:
'Tis how a brave man dies on the tree."

A Son of God was the Goodly Fere
That bade us his brothers be.
I ha' seen him cow a thousand men.
I have seen him upon the tree.

He cried no cry when they drave the nails
And the blood gushed hot and free,
The hounds of the crimson sky gave tongue
But never a cry cried he.

I ha' seen him cow a thousand men

On the hills o' Galilee,

They whined as he walked out calm between,

Wi' his eyes like the Grey o' the sea,

Like the sea that brooks no voyaging

With the winds unleashed and free,

Like the sea that he cowed at Genseret

Wi' twey words spoke' suddenly.

A master of men was the Goodly Fere,

A mate of the wind and sea,

If they think they ha' slain our Goodly Fere

They are fools eternally.

I ha' seen him eat o' the honey-comb

Sin' they nailed him to the tree.

Sandals in the Dust

Chapter I-Andrew Ben Jonah

Andrew, son of Jonah was born in Capernaum, Galilee, along the shores of the Harp shaped lake known as Genesserett or the Sea of Galilee. Born between 10 and 15 AD he was the younger brother of Simon, known as Peter. Andrew was the second youngest of the original 12. Andrew was, according to legend, the best friend of his cousin John who was the youngest of all the Apostles.

Andrew was raised to be a fisherman. His Father and his Brother Simon Peter was fisherman as well. The scripture mentions Andrew early in the Gospels as a follower of John the Baptist, who was his second cousin. This was where Andrew received his first call by the Master, to know Him. John the Baptist told Andrew and John "Behold the Lamb of God which takes away the sins of the World!" Andrew was called the second time in friendship when he went fishing with Simon and Jesus. The third call was to service when they left their fishing boats and followed Jesus to start his three-year ministry.

Andrew is always mentioned first in the lists of the Apostles and was featured in the feeding of the five thousand when he brought a boy with a lunch to Jesus. Andrew also brought Greeks to see Jesus making him the first real missionary of the twelve.

The ministry of Andrew after the resurrection is only written in legends and old writings. Most of them agree that Andrew went to Scythia first. While preaching in Scythia a young man of a rich and noble family joined him much against his family's wishes. While there an Angel was said to come to Andrew and order him to Ethiopia to help Matthew who was preaching there. When Andrew replied that he did not know the way the Angel told him to go to the Sea and get on the first ship he encountered. Andrew did this and helped with a divine wind, the ship quickly took Andrew to Africa where he made his way to Ethiopia and the prison that held Matthew.

It seems that Matthew had angered the Ethiopian village where he was preaching and they had burned his eyes and then cast him into prison. Andrew prayed and God miraculously healed the wounds of Matthew and restored his sight. Andrew immediately took Matthew to safety and then returned to this same village. The villagers were furious because of Matthews's escape and they beat and tortured Andrew for some time. According to the old writings, Andrew's testimony was so strong and his love for the people so sincere that they eventually were convinced to become followers of Jesus.

After establishing the church in this village, Andrew made his way to Greece. In Greece he established a house where he and the young nobleman mentioned above lived. The parents of this young man were so angry with Andrew that they set the house on fire. They then tried to use a ladder to climb up to a window and rescue the young man, but they were struck with blindness. While they fumbled about they cried and proclaimed that Andrew was a Sorcerer and that he had bewitched their son. A man who was watching the fire replied that they should be quiet and that could they not see the Angels of God fighting the fire. The fire was miraculously put out and many in the city believed in Jesus because of the witness of this miracle and the preaching of Andrew. As for the parents of the young follower of Andrew, they both died in their blindness about 50 days after the fire.

There was a certain woman in the city where Andrew lived who had married an assassin and was with child. Her labors began, but she could not after two days deliver the child. She begged her sister to go to the goddess Diana and pray for her help. Her sister went but instead of Diana, a demon answered and said that he had no power in this city and that the only help for the sister was from Andrew. The Sister lost no time in going to the house of Andrew and bringing him to the bedside of the woman in labor. The woman begged for help and Andrew replied: "You have ill married, ill conceived and then you have asked help of the Devil. Your only hope is to repent of your sins and trust in Jesus Christ as your only Savior from sin and death." After listening to the Gospel, the woman made a profession of faith and then the child was stillborn. Her pain and suffering were stopped but the consequences of her sin could not be undone.

There was an old man of about 70 years named Nicholas who had been an early follower of Andrew and came to him one day and said "Master, I love the Lord Jesus, but I have become so addicted to lust that it takes possession of my very soul. This very day after going out to witness the Gospel, I had a copy of Matthew's Gospel on my person and I forgot and entered the house of the temple prostitutes. I approached the mistress of the house when she began to wail and cry that I should leave as that I was a messenger of God and had no business in this place! I was amazed at her words when I realized that she had seen the Gospel I carried on my person. Master Andrew, can you help me?"

Andrew began to weep and immediately entered into prayer that lasted about 6 hours. He then rose and told Nicholas that he must fast and pray with him. Nicholas fasted on bread and water for the next 6 months leaving his bedroom only to pray with Andrew. He read the scriptures and prayed and worshiped God together with him daily. One day at the end of the 6 months when Andrew went to join in prayer with Nicholas, he found him asleep as he had passed away during the night. An Angel appeared and told Andrew to be at peace for Nicholas, for he was lost and now he was found.

About this time Andrew went to the town of Nicaea, there the people told him that there were 7 demons in the shape of wild dogs that guarded the city and had slain many.

Andrew called the seven spirits to him and they looked like wild dogs. He ordered them to depart for another city and they immediately left. Many people who had witnessed this miracle believed in the

Gospel of Jesus that Andrew preached unto them. Andrew then left and went to the next city where he found a man prostrate over the body of his only son that had been slain by the very same dogs Andrew had ordered out of Nicaea. Andrew was very grieved over his actions and cried unto the Lord for about an hour. He then asked the father what he would give him if God raised the son to life. The father answered "I have nothing of worth in my life other than my son, so if you restore his life, you may have him." Andrew took the young man buy his hand and his life returned unto him and the son immediately followed Andrew.

There were about 40 men who traveled by Sea to hear the preaching of Andrew. According to the ancient writings, Satan brought up a great storm and all of them perished. As the bodies were washed up on the beach of Patras, Andrew went to each one, prayed and lifted them up alive on the shore. A great crowd followed and with each miracle the rejoicing and fervor was greater and greater. After praying and restoring the life to the last man, Andrew summoned the crowd to come near and he preached the gospel to over 2,000 people. Many were saved and baptized in the sea that day and one of them was the wife of the Roman Proconsul Aegeus. The Proconsul came to the town of Patras and ordered all people to sacrifice to the Roman gods. Andrew met him and a great confrontation began. Aegeus told him that Jesus was nailed to a cross because He was weak and could not stop the Roman soldiers. Andrew gave him a five-part sermon as to why the Passion of Christ was voluntary. Now Andrew had been in this town and region by this time for over 25 years and had established many churches. Aegeus was angry about the churches and by the fact his own wife had left the gods and followed Jesus. The proconsul then warned Andrew that unless he ceased his preaching that he would find out exactly what the "Mystery of the Cross" was by experience. Andrew told the Proconsul that if he were afraid of the Cross-, he would have never preached in the first place.

There were many other words of debate but the end was that Aegeus was angry and ordered the Soldiers to crucify Andrew on an X shaped cross, which was more tortuous than the normal cross. This was due to the fact that there was no place to push up with the feet as they were spread out. Andrew was flogged and then led to the cross, which he approached without fear or cringing. The writings tell us that Andrew preached to over 20,000 people in the 2 days that he hung there till the people rushed the house of the Proconsul and threatened to kill him for daring to harm this blessed man. Andrew saw that they were rushing to take him down from the cross but he said, "Do not stop the Angels from taking me to be with my Lord, for I see the Heavens opened and Jesus standing at the right hand of God." The witnesses then saw a light from heaven surround Andrew and he died. The year was around 60AD. The wife of Aegeus took Andrew down and gave him a royal burial. Aegeus returned to the city but on the way to his house an Angel struck him and he died in the streets of Patras.

Sandals in the Dust

Chapter II-Simon Ben Jonah (Peter)

SIMON BEN JONAH

Simon Ben Jonah, better know as Simon Peter was born in Galilee about the same time or just after our Lord was born. He was born to Jonah, first cousin of Zebedee. It is important to note that while Peter and Andrew, his younger brother, were cousins to the Zebedee family, they were not related to Jesus, as were the Zebedee's. Perhaps more has been written about Peter than any other Apostle. He spent roughly the first half of his life as a fisherman. He spent the other half as a "Fisher of Men." Peter is mentioned often in all four of the gospels. He is always in the thick of every deed and as most people have already noticed, he seems to be a real man of action.

His first scene with Jesus is to take Him fishing. Understand that Peter knew Jesus personally when he asked him to go fishing that day. This was not a first meeting as many have supposed. The fact that he knew Jesus well and took Him out even though he had been up all night speaks volumes. Most of us would have told Jesus to come back later after we had slept. After this miraculous catch, of Fish Peter began

his new life. He was present when Jesus calmed the
Sea, present when Jesus brought the dead little girl to
life, present when Moses and Elijah appeared on the
mountain with Jesus and even took a short walk on
the Sea of Galilee with Jesus.

Peter wanted to know who the betrayer was in the
upper room. He probably would have done bodily
harm to him had Jesus revealed the name. He refused
to let Jesus wash his feet, at first, and then wanted a
bath! He was the first to fall asleep in the garden, but
also the first to take up the sword in our Master's
defense. He boldly followed to see what would
happen to Jesus before the High Priest and then
denied ever knowing Jesus at all immediately after.
Peter was a man of extremes. The most extreme
action he ever spoke of was to confess that Jesus was
"the Christ, the Son of the living God!" Then
alternatively tell Jesus that he would not allow him to
go to his death earning him a "get thee behind me,
Satan from our Savior.

Peter lost a running race with John to the tomb, but came away unbelieving just the same. His first action, after the resurrection, was to go fishing. Next come some of the more misinterpreted scriptures in our Gospels. Jesus asks Peter if he loves (Agape) Him. Peter replies "Yes Lord, I Love (Phileo) you. The Greek words here are very specific. Jesus asks Peter if he loves Him with the undying, all forgiving, unselfish Love of God. Peter being the man he was replies that he Loves Jesus like a Brother. Finally on the third time Jesus receives the response he desires and reminds Peter to be a Shepherd and feed the Sheep.

Peter was probably one of the least educated of all the disciples and John Mark wrote his account of the Gospel. Mark's Gospel is one of the easiest to read and is all action, sound like someone we know? Mark's mother had the prayer meeting when Peter was in Prison and was released by the Angel. Mark also made a missionary journey with Paul and

Barnabas, but later returned home. Paul was angry with Mark and did not want to take him on the second journey. Barnabas did and later so did Peter. According to legend when Peter was in Rome and wanted to write down the Gospel, it was Paul who recommended Mark to Peter. Paul even states in one of his later letters that Mark was profitable for ministry. Who more than Peter would believe in second chances?

Most of what I have related so far is found in the scriptures, but there is much more in the book of Acts by Luke about Peter. He was the first perform a miracle, first to preach to a large crowd, first to be beaten, first to be imprisoned. What many people do not know is that Peter's wife was killed when Herod imprisoned him. Simon Peter's wife is mentioned remotely in scripture. For Jesus to heal Peters Mother-in-law of a fever, Peter would have had to have a wife. There are two traditions of the death of Peter's wife. One is that she died in Jerusalem being killed by Herod. This was supposed to have happened when James the brother of John had returned from Spain. James lost his wife and children. The story is that Herod captured the families of James and Peter. He held them until both James and Peter came to confront him, as Herod knew they would. He imprisoned James and Peter, then killed the wives and children of both. One of Peter's daughters had been away and somehow escaped this. James was then killed with a sword. The rest of the story of the Angel leading Peter out of prison is well known from the scriptures.

After this incident there is a 25-year period of Peter's life of which the scriptures are not as detailed about Peter. Peter was said to have traveled to Rome to preach to people there. In fact, many scholars have theorized that the reason Paul did not want to go to Rome was because his old friend was already there. Peter is said to have established many churches and he appointed at least two Church leaders, Linus and Cletus. One was shepherd to the city and the other to the countryside around the city. Peter was said to arrive in Rome in the 4th year of Claudius's reign and stayed for over 25 years until his death.

Peter is quoted in some of the old writings as eating bread and olives only. He rarely also would have a few vegetables. His clothing was simple and it is said that he always carried a thick cloth or towel tucked in his belt. It is said that whenever he could remember the Master's words or remembered his betrayal that he would weep. He used the towel to dry his tears.

Peter is listed in the scriptures as becoming so powerful with the Spirit of God that his very shadow could heal. The stories of his healing of people are numerous. One such story is when he sent out two of his disciples, Maternas and George. While they were traveling, George sickened and died. Maternas went back to Peter to report what had happened. It had taken almost three weeks for George to return to Peter. Peter immediately gave his own staff to Maternas and told him to lay the staff on the body of

George and that he would live. Maternas immediately hurried back to the site of George's death. The body had been buried and Maternas dug it up. By this time it had been dead for over 40 days. Maternas laid the staff of Peter on the body and immediately George came back to life. Maternas and George had been preaching the northern village of the Italian Alps and the people were astonished. Many came to Christ as a result of this miracle and there is a church on the site of it unto this day.

No story of Peter could be told without talking of exactly what his role in the Church really was. There are many today that call him the first Pope. I realize that this is done out of veneration and respect and I have no reason to dispute the claims of one while I make another claim of my own. The importance of Peter was not in a building or in an organization, but in the Apostle himself. Known affectionately in literature as the "Big Fisherman" no one could argue the importance of Peter. In fact, except for the Apostle Paul who was killed in the same day by

Nero, no one dared to argue with Peter. He was a strong leader, who was humble enough to weep several times each day at the thought of his Master. He was absolutely fearless knowing that if an Angel saved him once, that God would continue to protect him until his work was done. He was tender with children remembering the words of his Master to "Feed my Lambs." He owned no property, carried no money and never wanted for a meal or shelter until his death. Peter was in Rome, when Linus sent him a letter from Jerusalem about Simon the Sorcerer. Simon was on his way to Rome to see Nero. Paul had just been given liberty from his first hearing with Nero. Peter asked Paul to join him in the showdown before Nero with Simon.

Peter had come to Rome in the first place because Simon had left Jerusalem and traveled to Rome. As you may recall, Simon had attempted to purchase the power of the Holy Spirit from Peter and was harshly rebuked. Some scholars speculate that Simon wanted to go somewhere away from the power of the

Apostles and when Peter heard that Simon went to Rome, he felt led of God to Follow him. Peter did arrive in Rome about 39 AD.

The Last couple of years of Peter's ministry were entirely to witness to Nero against the witchcraft and sorcery of Simon. It is recorded in the old writings that God spoke to Peter through an Angel and said: "I know that Nero and Simon have evil designs upon you, but fear not. I shall send my servant Paul to comfort and strengthen thee." Paul, having been released from prison the first time and traveled to see some of his churches, was arriving in Rome that very day. Never has the servants of Satan had two more powerful foes!

Simon the Sorcerer had become so important to Nero, that by this time many of the city's inhabitants felt that Simon held the fate of Rome in his hands. One day while Simon was in the presence of Nero he changed his appearance so that one minute he looked like a young man, the next an old man. Nero was so impressed that he declared Simon a god and had a statue made of him for people to worship. Simon even tricked Nero into thinking that he was beheaded and that he arose after three days. Nero lost all doubts about the divinity of Simon.

Peter and Paul entered Nero's court and exposed Simon to the Emperor. They said the difference between Jesus and Simon was that Jesus was both divine and human, but Simon was human and diabolical. Nero was unconvinced and Peter proposed a test where he would whisper a secret to Nero and that Simon must read his thoughts. Peter whispered that a Barley loaf should be brought secretly to Peter so that he could bless it. The bread was brought and Peter hid it in his sleeve. Simon was so ashamed that he said that in all fairness that Peter and Paul should read his thoughts first. Peter said, "I already have." When Simon released from the door several large, hungry dogs leaped at Peter and Paul. Peter took the bread from his sleeve and threw it to the dogs that immediately ate the bread and then cuddled at the feet of everyone but Simon who left the room in a rage. The dogs chased him and ripped his clothes off his body so that he ran home naked and ashamed. Many were made believers by this showing of God's power over Satan.

Simon finally made one final showdown between Peter and Paul. He climbed to the highest point in the city and Jumped into the air and flew. People from one end of Rome to the other witnessed this and Nero told Peter and Paul that they were false while Simon was true. Peter being grieved looked up and spoke these words. "Angels of Satan who hold this man in the air. I command you in the name of my Master, Jesus Christ, to hold him up no longer!" Without the help of the demons, Simon fell rather quickly and died in the streets of Rome. Nero was angry and called his advisors while Peter and Paul left his presence.

Peter had decided to go back to Jerusalem and see his fellow church members again when he saw Jesus coming towards him. Peter was astonished and asked what was happening. Jesus told Peter that he would have to take his place and die again with Paul. Peter immediately turned around and Jesus was gone. Peter knew that the Master was telling him to return to Nero's presence. Now Paul was a Roman citizen and Peter was not. When they both returned to speak to Nero, they were immediately taken and led towards their deaths. Peter was taken to be crucified, as legend tells us, he asked to be crucified upside down as he said he was not worthy to die like Jesus. Paul on the same day was taken to the executioner, being Roman, and was beheaded. Peter and Paul died the same day on 64AD. The Church under Clement in Rome took their bodies and buried them where they can be seen unto this day.

Sandals in the Dust

Chapter III-James Ben Zebedee

James the son of Zebedee was an older brother to John, first cousin to the sons of Jonah through his father and the sons of Alpheus through his mother and first cousin of our Lord Jesus as well. James was about the same age of Peter and followed Jesus when he was in his early thirties. James was married according to some traditions. James was a leader of the Apostles who was always present in the inner circle of Jesus' followers with John and of course Peter. James witnessed the raising of the synagogue ruler's daughter from death, the appearance of Moses and Elijah on the mountain and the agony of Christ in the Garden.

There are no significant acts or deeds of James recorded in the scriptures save the occasion when he and his brother John wanted call fire down from heaven to burn up the unbelievers. Obviously the quiet James had steel beneath the calm exterior. Jesus of course rebuked him and John for their lack of compassion. Yet we see that Jesus kept him close at all times. James, unlike Peter, was a man who spoke little, but did much. When he followed Christ, he followed in silence. When he doubted the resurrection, he doubted in silence. After the resurrection, James was said to have preached in Judea and Samaria. While he was preaching, one of his children was said to have been killed by a drunken Roman soldier. James was so grieved that he and his cousin Barsabas or Joseph the Just boarded the first ship leaving Caesarea. This ship was bound for an Island off the coast of present day Tunisia called Djerba.

On this Island, there was and still is a large population of Cohen or Levite priests. Many of them had settled there before the captivity of Babylon. It is rumored by some that the Ark of the Covenant and other Temple treasures are guarded there waiting for Israel's return and the restoration of the Temple which was destroyed about 70AD but was still in existence at this time. James and Barsabas began to share in the synagogue each Yom Shabbat or Saturday. The Jewish people of this Island became very angry and threatened to stone James. Barsabas put him on a ship sailing for Galatia or present-day Spain.

Barsabas is an interesting character in the New Testament. Brother of James, Jude and Simon Alpheus, he was first mentioned by Luke in the Acts of the Apostles. From this election, we see a summary of both men. Barsabas according to legend was the outright favorite of Apostles. He had followed Jesus with them since the beginning. He had witnessed the crucifixion and resurrection of our Lord Jesus. He was among those who received the gift of the Holy Spirit on the day of Pentecost. Matthias was chosen and according to legend, Barsabas continued to be a strong witness of Christ. The Jews stoned Barsabas on the Island of Djerba. James sailed to Spain and began a missionary journey that is largely unrecorded. The record tells us that in several years that James had only 9 converts.

James is said to have preached and traveled wearing his old fishing hat. Above the rim he had several scallop shells attached. James was a simple man but he covered a lot of ground. Being a fisherman all those years told him that if the fish are not biting, it might be time to move on.

James followed a path to the cities of La Linea on the coast. From there he traveled to Hispalis, Cordoba, Merida, Saragossa, Vienna in the far northern reaches of Spain, Leon, Astorga and finally Compostela which is today know as Santiago de Compostela or St James of Compostela. There is one ancient writer who states that there was only one convert during all of this time, but most writers agree on the nine.

At this time around 40AD, word reached James that the rest of his family along with the family of Peter was being held by Herod in prison. James left two of his followers to minister to the fledgling mission and asked 7 to return with him to Jerusalem. He made the voyage to Jerusalem in record time. A witch in the hire of Abiathar, the High Priest, immediately confronted him at this time. Hermogenes was a magician who was said to have studied under Simon the Magician. He sent his student Philetus to confront James and to get evidence of false doctrine to use against him and the other Apostles.

As James reasoned with Philetus, he also was ministering to the crowd and performed many miracles as he was talking. Philetus was converted. He returned to Hermogenes and recounted the doctrine, miracles and that he intended to become a disciple of James. Hermogenes was so angered that he cast a demonic spell on Philetus so that he could not move. He then sent a messenger to James to tell him what he had done and to see if James would come to rescue Philetus. James sent his handkerchief with the following blessing: "The Lord lifts up them that fall and sets the captive free!" No sooner than Philetus had the handkerchief put in his hand; he was healed and immediately kept repeating the blessing of James. Philetus hurried to the side of James and returned the handkerchief.

Hermogenes was so angered that he conjured a demon to come forth and do his bidding. He ordered the demon to apprehend James and Philetus and return them in chains. As the demons were flying through the air they came close and saw the Apostle James. They immediately started crying out and said: "Apostle James, have pity on us, for we burn before our time." James replied: "To what end are you here?" The demons replied: "We are bound with chains and are to wrap you in these same chains and return you to Hermogenes that he may torture you." The Apostle immediately told the demons: "I will release you on one condition, that you bring Hermogenes to me unharmed.

 The demons immediately captured Hermogenes and cursed him and beat him and begged James to allow them to avenge themselves upon him. James asked them why they did not attempt to seize Philetus and they replied: "We cannot as much as touch the ant in his or your house." James then turned to Philetus and asked him what Christ would do. Philetus said: "Christ would return good for evil." James commanded the demons to put Hermogenes down and to depart. After they were gone Hermogenes cowered before James afraid of God's power in him. James told him to leave, as he could not convert an unwilling man. Hermogenes said that he could not leave unless James gave something of his to him to protect him from the vengeance of the demons. James gave Hermogenes his Staff.

Hermogenes went home and gathered all of his books and articles used in his magic. He brought it to James and fell at his feet and prayed to God: "You, who have set souls free, please receive this penitent man and may I have forgiveness for seeking harm against your children." James took all of the items used for magic and cast them into the Sea. Word was sent back to Abiathar, the High Priest, that both Hermogenes and Philetus were disciples of James.

As you can imagine, Abiathar was not pleased with the news and he sent word to Herod that James and Peter were stirring up the people. Herod had already killed the families of James and Peter and was waiting for them to willingly appear before him, as he knew they would. Both Peter and James were caught with ropes and were dragged by the neck to Herod's Palace. One of Abiathar's servants who were dragging the rope of James noticed that he was riding near a blind beggar on the street. Trying to topple the man with the body of James, he rode very close. James reached out and touched the man as he was being dragged by. The man immediately received his sight and began to praise God. The servant was so moved that he stopped, took the rope off of James and knelt at his feet. He prayed for forgiveness and to become of follower of Jesus.

Abiathar was furious with his servant. He had his hands bound behind him and told him to spit and curse the name of Jesus and that he would be set free.

The servant refused. Abiathar then sent to Herod and received permission for the servant to be killed with the other two prisoners. As you well know Peter was to be killed on Easter Sunday, James was to be killed on the Friday before. James took the servant into the brook when they stopped for water, and he baptized him. Peter was a witness. Peter and James were separated at this time, never in this life to see each other again. The servant, whose name is not recorded, except in the book of life, was never named and was beheaded on the same day as James.

As you read this story about Peter being miraculously released by an Angel from prison. James is killed or martyred. The age-old question is why? The brother of James, John, wrote in his Gospel, Chapter 12, the following: "Truly I say to you, unless a kernel of wheat falls to the ground and dies, it lives alone. But if it dies, it produces much fruit." John was quoting Jesus before he went to be crucified. But was Jesus only talking about himself? If the Apostles were willing to follow Jesus even unto death, then like the seed planted in fertile ground, much fruit would follow.

James in about three years of ministry had only converted 9 converts. After his death and return to Spain, thousands of people would become Christians and by the end of the first century, seven major churches would be spread across the entire region with hundreds of smaller ones.

On March 25, 44 AD, Herod had James beheaded with a Roman sword. His seven Spanish disciples were afraid for their lives and retrieved his body and put it in a ship.

Legend tells us that with out a course or a rudder they sailed wanting God to reveal where the body of James should be laid to rest. After many days of sailing, the ship landed on the Spanish shores of Galatia. A queen named Lupa or she-wolf, which was a name well deserved by her reputation, ruled this land. The disciples laid the body on a large stone that immediately became as hot wax. The stone miraculously shaped itself into a sarcophagus that fitted itself to the body of James. The Disciples then went to Queen Lupa and said: "Our Lord Jesus sends you the body of his Apostle that you may welcome him in death whom you would not welcome alive." The disciples of James then told the story of how God had guided them to her and about the miraculous stone sarcophagus. They then asked for burial place for their master.

Queen Lupa, hoping to deceive them sent them to the King of Spain. Now the King was known to be a harsh and cruel man and he immediately cast all seven of the disciples into prison. That night as the king slept, an Angel of the Lord released the disciples and they immediately left for the body of James once again. The king awoke on the morning and learned of their escape. He sent soldiers out to re-capture the disciples. The soldiers were within sight of them when crossing a bridge. The bridge collapsed and all of them perished. The King was then afraid and sent word to the disciples that they should return and that he would do whatever they desired. When the disciples returned they told the King their whole story and the King repented of his sins and were converted.

Soon the entire city followed their king in proclaiming Christ as their Savior. The disciples went once again to Queen Lupa and told her that the King had given them permission to build a church around the grave of James. Queen Lupa once again full of deception told them to go the nearby mountain pasture and yoke the oxen there and use them to carry the tomb of James where they will. The Queen knew that these were wild oxen that had never been yoked and she hoped they would kill the disciples. The disciples took her at her word and went and found the oxen that acted as gentle as a lamb. The disciples returned to the Queen's palace with the sarcophagus and carried it right into the palace. Queen Lupa was so astounded at the actions of these wild animals that she realized that this must be of God. She immediately repented and became a Christian and gave the palace to the disciples to use as a church.

This palace became the first official Christian church in Spain. Today it is know as Santiago de Compostela or the tomb of St James. The Apostle James Converted more souls to Christianity by being martyred.

Sandals in the Dust

Part IV-James Ben Alpheus

James the son of Alpheus or James Ben Alpheus is one of the most legendary of all the minor Apostles. Much has been written about him and attributed to him that is unread and unknown of today. From Jerome to Josephus, Philo or Clement, James is written about and known of in history as well as the Bible.

One of the reasons James is such a remembered character is that he is often represented as James the brother of our Lord. There are several reasons for this confusion. James was a first cousin of Jesus from his mother's side. His mother named Mary was a half-sister to Mary the mother of Jesus. As we have dealt with already, both Mary's have different fathers, but the same mother. So we have genetics as reason number one why James resembled Jesus so closely. Reason number tow is a cultural reason. Alpheus the father of James was a younger brother to Joseph, the stepfather of Jesus. Both Jesus and James were raised as the sons of carpenters. Aside from Jesus' families sojourn in Egypt, they were raised in Galilee and had similar customs of hair and clothing. Reason number three was a spiritual reason. James followed Jesus for three years learning to emulate him spiritually just as we attempt to do today. The Scripture bears out the family relation of James to John and Jesus in the Gospel of John when the two Mary's were standing together at the cross.

According to most of the ancient writings, whenever Jesus was with the two sons of Zebedee and Peter, James Alpheus was in charge of the other group. In fact, one story of scripture is really brought to light by the knowledge of what James Alpheus looked like. According to the Golden Legend and other sources, the High Priest and others in Jerusalem had trouble telling Jesus and James Alpheus apart. Apparently they being from the same family they dressed very similarly and wore their hair and beard in the same manner.

When the priests bribed Judas Iscariot to betray Jesus, they wanted to make sure that it was really Jesus that they apprehended since it was an illegal arrest anyway. They instructed Judas that the only difference in looks was the eye color, Jesus had blue eyes according to tradition and James Alpheus had brown. If they took Jesus by night they could not be sure of the eyes so they told Judas to greet Jesus with a kiss so they could not be mistaken.

 Of course the priests could not know that Jesus would have come willingly and that this was God's plan for him. They assumed that Jesus would allow his "twin" to be taken in His place. They were so frightened of Jesus that when He said "I Am He" they jumped back and hit the ground as if expecting some great attack. James Alpheus of course knew that Jesus would never allow him to be taken in His place.

There are several examples of scriptures where Jesus simply walked away from an angry crowd. Not being sure who to stone may have facilitated this to ensure that God's plan of salvation on the Cross was fulfilled.

James had by far the most spiritual discipline of any Apostle. He prayed so often and so long that legend tells us that his knees were like the knees of Camels, very thick and callused. When our Lord Ascended into Heaven and the Church began in Jerusalem, the Apostles prayed for guidance from the Holy Spirit as to who should go where. James looking so much like Jesus must have been a painful reminder to all in Jerusalem of what they had done to our Savior. Even still, when someone was chosen to lead the Church in Jerusalem, James was chosen to do so and did this for over 30 years.

It was during this time that he wrote the Epistle of James, which you can find in your Bible. There are some who credit this book with the actual half-brother of Jesus named James or someone else entirely. There are some that believe that Mary had no other children other than Jesus and that the Aramaic word for Cousin and Brother cause the confusion on this part. Most of the ancient sources do credit this book to James Alpheus.

James Ben Alpheus was chosen to be the Pastor of the Church in Jerusalem. Most of the other Apostles were traveling from place to place with the Gospel leaving James to run what was probably the most difficult Church in the first century World.

It was made difficult by several reasons: One, the Jews in Jerusalem had crucified Christ and was still among the most vocal critiques of the new faith. Two, James looked so much like Jesus that he must have been a constant reminder to everyone that he met of reason number one. Three, the high priests of Jerusalem had a pretty good arrangement going with Rome and the people and were left with positions of power as long as the people continued to pay homage to them. Christianity was an inroad into this authority and this is why they continued to fight it so combatively. I wonder if it would have been easier for James to have left this place and take the gospel to an unknown land than to stay put for over 30 years. Obviously James was exactly where God wanted him.

James Ben Alpheus has been credited by many historical authors including Jerome and Josephus as being the prime reason for the destruction of the Temple by the Romans around 70 AD. James' preaching was causing such uproar that he was challenged by The Jews, being exasperated at the disappointment of their malicious designs against Paul, by his appeal to Caesar, to whom he was sent by Festus, in the year 60, were resolved to revenge it on James.

That governor, dying before the arrival of his successor, Albinus, this vacancy gave them an opportunity of acting more arbitrarily than otherwise they would have done. Wherefore, during this interval, Ananus, the high priest, son of the famous Annas mentioned in the gospels, having assembled the great council of the Jews summoned James and others before it. Josephus, the Jewish historian, says that James was accused of violating the laws, and was delivered to the people to be stoned to death.

Hegesippus adds that they carried him up to the battlements of the temple, and would have hurled him from there to make a public renunciation of his faith in Christ, with this further view, thereby to undeceive, as they termed it, those among the people who had embraced Christianity. But James took that opportunity to declare his belief in Jesus Christ, after the most solemn and public manner. For he cried out aloud from the battlements, in the hearing of a great multitude, which was then at Jerusalem on account of the Passover, that Jesus, the Son of man, was seated at the right hand of the Sovereign Majesty, and would come in the clouds of heaven to judge the world.

The Scribes and Pharisees, enraged at this testimony in behalf of Jesus, cried out: "The just man also hath erred." And going up to the battlements, they threw him headlong down to the ground, saying, "He must be stoned." James, though very much bruised by his fall, had strength enough to get upon his knees, and in this posture, lifting up his eyes to heaven, he begged of God to pardon his murderers, seeing that they knew not what they did.

The rabble below received him with showers of stones, and at last a fuller gave him a blow on the head with his club, such as is used in dressing of cloths, after which he presently expired. This happened on the festival of the Pasch, the 10th of April, in the year of Christ 62, the seventh of Nero.

He was buried near the temple, in the place in which he was martyred, where a small column was erected. Such was the reputation of his sanctity that the Jews attributed to his death the destruction of Jerusalem, as we read in Jerome, Origen, and Eusebius who assure us that Josephus himself declared it in the genuine editions of his history. Ananus put others to death for the same cause, but was threatened for this very fact by Albinus, and deposed from the high priesthood by

Agrippa. Of course the Romans may have used this riot as an excuse to start the campaign that did eventually eradicate the Temple.

The church in Jerusalem would continue for many years with others filling in as Pastor, but in all the old writings, there were none to compare to the zeal, the holiness and the wisdom of James Ben Alpheus.

Sandals in the Dust

Chapter V-Jude Ben Alpheus

No story of Jude Ben Alpheus could be complete without telling you of his secret mission from Jesus himself. Jude was the brother to James and Simon and is mentioned as one of the brothers of Christ. Understand that the meaning of the word brother in the ancient languages can well mean a cousin. In the gospels when the people of Cana are confronted with Jesus during the ministry they mention all three brothers as rational as to why Jesus cannot be divine. How wrong they were. The following story has been translated in the 15th century and is counted by many including Jerome to be true.

The legend, according to these two works, runs as follows: Abgar, king of Edessa, afflicted with an incurable sickness, has heard the fame of the power and miracles of Jesus and writes to Him, praying Him to come and heal him. Jesus declined, but promised to send a messenger, endowed with His power, namely Thaddeus (or Jude Ben Alpheus), one of the seventy-two Disciples and one of the chosen Apostles. The letters of our Lord and of the king of Edessa vary in the version given in Eusebius and in that of the "Teaching of Addaï or Jude." That which follows is taken from the Teaching of Addaï," as being less accessible than the History of Eusebius:

Abgar Ouchama to Jesus, the Good Physician Who as appeared in the country of Jerusalem, greeting: I have heard of Thee, and of Thy healing; that thou dost not use medicines or roots, but by Thy word opens (the eyes) of the blind, makes the lame to walk, cleanses the lepers, makes the deaf to hear; how by Thy word (also) Thou heals (sick) spirits and those who are tormented with lunatic demons, and how, again, Thou raises the dead to life. And, learning the wonders that Thou doest, it was borne in upon me that (of two things, one): either Thou hast come down from heaven, or else Thou art the Son of God, who brings all these things to pass. Wherefore I write to Thee, and pray that thou wilt come to me, who adore Thee, and heal all the ill that I suffer, according to the faith I have in Thee. I also learn that the Jews murmur against Thee, and persecute Thee, that they seek to crucify Thee, and to destroy Thee. I possess but one small city, but it is beautiful, and large enough for us two to live in peace.

When Jesus had received the letter, in the house of the high priest of the Jews, He said to Hannan, the secretary, "Go thou, and say to thy master, who hath sent thee to Me: 'Happy art thou who hast believed in Me, not having seen me, for it is written of me that those who shall see me shall not believe in Me, and that those who shall not see Me shall believe in Me. As to that which thou hast written, that I should come to thee, (behold) all that for which I was sent here below is finished, and I ascend again to My Father who sent Me, and when I shall have ascended to Him I will send thee one of My disciples, who shall heal all thy sufferings, and shall give (thee) health again, and shall convert all who are with thee unto life eternal. And thy city shall be blessed forever, and the enemy shall never overcome it.'" According to Eusebius, it was not Hannan, who wrote answer, but our Lord Himself.

According to legend, Jude traveled to modern southern Turkey, where the Kingdom of Edessa once existed, and brought a handkerchief with the image of Jesus on it. The King was healed of his disease and was converted to Christianity. Jude returned to Jerusalem without ever mentioning this commission fulfilled. Eusebius found his record in his own writings in the fourth century. We know from history that this story really did happen and the Mandilion or image of Christ resides with the Shroud of Turin in Edessa to this day.

The Mandilion

First we started with the secret mission of Jude which concluded with him preaching to the entire city of Edessa. After Jude returned from this mission, Thomas appointed two Apostles to go to the middle-east. Simon went to Egypt, Jude to Mesopotamia.

There are no records surviving to tell us the details of these trips but it is important to note that these places were reached with the Gospel long before North America. Simon who was south in Egypt went north up into Persia or modern Iran. Jude who was in Modern Iraq joined Simon in Iran. Two magicians who had been run out of Ethiopia by Matthew confronted them. Their names were Zaroes and Arphaxat according to the Golden Legend. There was also a captain of the Babylonian Army known as Baradach. Baradach was consulting his gods as to the wisdom of attacking India who had refused tribute to Babylon. When the idols could not answer him in his city, he went to a neighboring city and was told by the gods that they could not answer because the Apostles Jude and Simon had come to the city.

The Captain sought out the Apostles and asked them "Who are you, where do you come from and why?" The Apostles answered: "If you ask us our race, we are Hebrew. If you ask us our condition, we are servants of Christ. If you are asking the reason of our visit, it is to bring you Salvation." The Captain replied: "When I have returned victorious from battle, I shall hear you." The Apostles answered: "It would be better for you to hear us before you go and save yourself much effort and many lives." The Captain then wanted the Apostles to foretell the outcome of his war and they told him to bring the sorcerers in and ask them first. Zaroes and Arphaxat then predicted a great battle and victory for the Captain to which the Apostles began to laugh.

The Captain was alarmed at their laughter but they told him that it would be ridiculous to attack an Army that was sending at that moment an envoy to pay tribute and ask for peace under the rule of Babylon. The Captain then put both the magicians and the Apostles under guard for the night to await the results. The next morning, the peace envoy from India did arrive and do exactly as the Apostles said. The Captain wanted to put the magicians to death but the Apostles stayed his hand saying: "We have come to bring life, not death to your people."

At this time news came that the Apostles were wanted back in Jerusalem. The people begged them to stay so Jude stayed and Simon returned to Jerusalem. (We shall continue his story later) Jude preached and taught many thousands of the people of Babylon and converted over 60,000 converts not including the women and children. He appointed teachers and Deacons to lead the church.

About this time a woman was with child and was not married. When the baby was born she went to the church to ask the Deacon to bless the baby. The Deacon told her to find the baby's father and return that they may be married. The woman not knowing who the father was told him that she would tell everyone in the city that the baby was his unless he blessed her baby.

News of the "indiscretion" of the Deacon spread like fire throughout the city. Calming the mob, Jude asked the woman with child to come forward. Jude then looked at this newborn baby and asked him to tell if the Deacon was his father. The Baby replied that the Deacon was holy and had never defiled his flesh and was not his father.

The people were amazed at this miracle and asked the Apostle to ask the baby who the father was. The apostle replied that he was there to free the innocent, not to shackle the guilty.

Many people were converted to Christ because of the miracle of the talking newborn. Jude continued for many years to preach and teach the whole twelve provinces of Persia and taught in Syria, Lebanon, and in Babylon.

If you read the letter of Jude, which is in the New Testament, you will find that the Apostle Peter seems to be familiar with it as well in II Peter. It was written around 66 or 67 AD. The fact that this small letter had so much history and knowledge would be well supported by the fact that the Church in Persia and Syria was over 100,000 people strong by the middle of the first century. Many would have had copies of it, which increases the opportunity for us to read it today, which we do in the New Testament.

According to tradition, Jude was martyred in Beirut Lebanon in about AD 65. Some of the oldest representations of him show a halberd or Axe as the instrument of his Death. While the details of Jude's Death have been lost, his tracks in the dust of time have still not faded.

Sandals in the Dust

Chapter VI-Simon Ben Alpheus

We started the story of Simon Ben Alpheus in the middle, so I think It would be wise to go back to the beginning. Simon, like his three brothers and father, was a carpenter. He was a man that liked to work with wood.

Unlike frame carpenters who liked to make houses, Simon was a man that could look at a piece of wood and see dishes or tables or cabinets, such as they were in that day. Simon liked to carve wood into shapes, but being Jewish, he never carved wood into animate objects as could be construed as an idol. He especially liked to make toys for children and even when he reached 120 years of age, he was still making small toys for the children of the Church in Jerusalem.

As you can imagine, this made Simon very popular with all of the Children. Some writings tell us that Simon was the oldest of all the Apostles when he followed Jesus. This is why John who was the youngest could live to be almost 100 years of age and still outlast Simon who was 20 years or so older. Apart from John, who died a natural death at 100 or more, Simon lived longer than any of the apostles and is thought to be the oldest person ever to endure crucifixion by the Romans.

Simon is called Zelotes in the scriptures. This word would be translated Zealot or one with great zeal. Many have thought that Simon was among those who wanted to overthrow the Romans called Zealots.

Patriots, Freedom Fighters, call them what you will but nobody can blame them for wanting the Romans out of their Country. Many believe that Simon and Judas Iscariot were both members of this sect that was led by Barabbas. In the popular movie King of Kings, Judas and Simon are both hoping that Jesus will become the King and with his Power from God, will overthrow the Romans with just a word. Isidore and others of old believe that Judas wanted Jesus to be Messiah so badly that he betrayed Him to the Pharisees hoping that Jesus when threatened would defend himself. This is where Simon and Judas parted company. Simon would not betray the Master no matter what good could come of it and said no.

Judas acts alone and only later realizes that he is wrong and hangs himself. Barabbas is released instead of Jesus and he decides that Simon has been right all along and becomes a disciple according to some writings. No matter what Simon's political views were, after following Jesus for three years, they were changed forever. His Zeal would become transformed into being as much like the Master, Jesus, as he possibly could.

As we have said before, Simon and his brother Jude was both assigned missionary works in the Middle East. When their brother James was cast from the Temple roof and killed, they were both summoned to return to Jerusalem where a council of remaining Apostles would be held and a new Pastor to lead the flock of Jerusalem and the world-wide effort would be chosen. Jude knew that his brother Simon was a perfect candidate for this position and refused to return, but instead gave his blessing to his brother, according to Isadore's "Life of the Apostles", and stayed behind as we have said. Simon would not see his brother again on this Earth. His brother Barsabas had died in northern Africa with James Zebedee, His Brother James martyred by the people of Jerusalem and now as he arrives in Jerusalem himself, word reaches him that the church in Jerusalem has gone into hiding.

Simon's first act was to go to the house of Mary, mother of John Mark, whose house had been used as a Church many times in the past and was the place of Peter knocking at the door with the Maid called Rhoda in the book of Acts. Once he arrived he sent messengers to all the homes of the believers from Galilee to Antioch. After time in Prayer and after a memorial service for James, the church met to select a new leader. Simon was the unanimous choice of the believers and he would remain in this position for the next 50 odd years.

Simon Ben Alpheus has just been selected to fill the toughest role in the first-century Church. Jerusalem would suffer many things during the pastorate of Simon. In 70 AD, Titus led a group of Romans to destroy the Temple of Jerusalem. Time and time again, this Temple had become the center of controversial movements. In many of the old writings, it is reported that a movement in Rome had begun to destroy this temple soon after the crucifixion of Jesus.

Reports of Pilate giving in to the mob and handing over an innocent man (Jesus) had filtered back to Rome. Caesar had demanded that Pilate come to Rome to answer for his deeds. Pilate wrote many letters to Rome to try and defend his actions but was finally replaced and after returning to Rome was put to death for his actions. The death of James at the Temple was the final straw. It was reported that every riot and unruly deed was always in the shadow of this Temple.

To Simon, this must have been a bittersweet event. Simon had read the words that Jesus that he spoke to the Samaritan woman at the well; "Neither in Jerusalem nor on this mountain will men worship God." He knew that the temple was no longer necessary, that the veil, a garment that would hold 4 horses together running in four opposite directions, had been rent in two because of Jesus, and what He did on the Cross, Man now had access directly to God.

However, being Jewish, how sad it must have been to see the place where his Master had walked and taught being torn down, not one brick left standing, all of the temple relics being carried away like so much loot. How hard it must have been to convince his flock that Jesus said we must love our enemies, and render to Caesar that which was Caesars.

By this time stories of the murder of Apostles and believers were coming in from all over the world on a daily basis. Of the original 12, by 70 AD, only a few remained. Paul and Peter both killed on the same day by Nero. All of his brothers killed for the Gospel. By the end of the century, during the reign of Trajan, only the Apostle John remained and he was in Ephesus in Asia Minor. It may have been the effect of so many deaths or the Zeal of a man who had become so much like Jesus, but it is written by John Beleth in "The Summa" that Simon raised over 30 dead men back to life so that they could continue to serve our Lord.

By this time Christianity had spread to most of the known world and reached from England in the west to China in the east. He saw the great commission fulfilled in his lifetime.

Finally when Simon was about 120 years of age, the new Consul named Atticus had Simon seized and tortured. Many marveled that so old a man could take this kind of torture, but Simon endured it without a whimper for many days. Finally, in a rage, Atticus commanded Simon to be crucified. Simon, at the age of 120 years, was nailed to a tree in Jerusalem in the same place of our Lord. Simon is rumored to have had supernatural strength that allowed him to resist suffocation for many days. Finally Atticus had him taken down and beheaded. The legend tells us that Simon resisted being taken down because he kept saying that he wanted to be like Jesus. It took only three soldiers to Crucify Simon, it took over 15 soldiers to take him down.

After the death of Simon the Church went on, like it always does with leadership falling to the Apostle John who traveled to Jerusalem and then visited many of the other churches as well until his exile to the Isle of Patmos which is another story. Reading about the death of Simon has always had an effect on me.

Whether he was crucified or behead with a Halberd, I believe he was as much like Jesus as a man could hope to be in this life. It is easy to ask, "What would Jesus do?" Simon saw what Jesus did and tried to be just like Him. I believe he succeeded.

Sandals in the Dust

Chapter VII-Phillip Ben Tolomai

Phillip Ben Tolomai was raised in Galilee near our Savior. He, his Father and brother were tanners and tent makers. From their herds of goats and sheep they made the tents that were used by the people of Israel for their feasts and for living. Many of these skins were also used for clothing articles such as belts and sandals.

Phillip, whose name is also spelled Philip, was an early disciple of John the Baptist along with John Zebedee and Andrew Jonah. He was instrumental in introducing his brother Nathaniel, He is also known as Bartholomew, to Jesus. Phillip was the one who brought the boy with the lunch to Jesus for the miracle of the fish and bread that fed over 20,000 people. It was the men who were counted as 5000; this did not include the women and children present. Phillip was a leader among the first century church in the field.

When a large group of missionaries that included Lazarus, Mary Magdalene and Joseph of Arimathea went west to Gaul and Britain, Phillip was charged to lead this mission team. Joseph of Arimathea was a wealthy disciple of Jesus, who, according to the book of Matthew 27:57-60, asked Pontius Pilate for permission to take Jesus' dead body in order to prepare it for burial. He also provided the tomb where the crucified Lord was laid until his Resurrection. Joseph is mentioned in a few times in parallel passages in Mark, Luke and John, but nothing further is heard about his later activities.

Apocryphal legend, however, supplies us with the rest of his story by claiming that Joseph accompanied the Apostle Philip, Lazarus, Mary Magdalene & others on a preaching mission to Gaul. Lazarus & Mary stayed in Marseilles, while the others traveled north. At the English Channel, Phillip sent Joseph, with twelve disciples, to establish Christianity in the most far-flung corner of the Roman Empire: the Island of Britain. The year AD 63 is commonly given for this event.

It was said that Joseph achieved his wealth in the metals trade, and in the course of conducting his business, he probably became acquainted with Britain, at least the southwestern parts of it. Cornwall was a chief mining district and well known in the Roman Empire for its tin. Somerset was renowned for its high quality lead. Some have even said that Joseph was the uncle of Mary the mother of Jesus and therefore of Jesus and that he may have brought the young boy along on one of his business trips to the island. This would have occurred after the death of Joseph the father of Jesus. Hence the words of Blake's famous hymn, Jerusalem:

And did those feet, in ancient time,
Walk upon England's mountains green?

Joseph of Arimathea and the Thorn Tree in England

It was only natural, then, that Joseph should have been chosen for the first mission to Britain, and appropriate that he should come first to Glastonbury, that gravitational center for legendary activity in the West Country. Local legend has it that Joseph sailed around Land's End and headed for his old lead mining haunts. Here his boat ran ashore in the Glastonbury Marshes and, together with his followers, he climbed a nearby hill to survey the surrounding land. Having brought with him a staff grown from Christ's Holy Crown of Thorns, he thrust it into the ground and announced that he and his twelve companions were "Weary All".

The thorn staff immediately took miraculous root, and it can be seen there still on Wearyall Hill. Joseph met with the local ruler, Aviragus, and soon secured himself twelve hides of land at Glastonbury on which to build the first Church in Britain. From here he became the First evangelist and missionary of England.

Much more was added to Joseph's legend. He was said to have brought with him a Cup used at the Last Supper. Many of the people in Jerusalem had started putting almost "Idol" status to this cup and Joseph wanted this put to a stop. He is said to have found an abandoned lead mine in Cornwall and to have buried the cup there. There have been many movies made and much literature written about the "Holy Grail." As you can see, this cup had nothing to do with the sacrifice made on the cross and Joseph wanted to make sure that nothing detracted from the Gospel. Is the cup of Christ still buried in England today? Did the legendary knights of King Arthur find this cup? To these questions we will never know for sure, but one thing is sure, Phillip had a hand in the evangelizing of Britain and France. He then later joined his Brother Nathaniel on a trip to what is now known as Turkey.

When Phillip or Philip (Depends on the school) returned from England and France from his missionary endeavors there, history tells us that he and his brother went to the coastal areas of what is now modern Turkey. From what we read about Phillip in the New Testament, Phillip introduced Jesus to his Brother Nathaniel and Jesus called him to follow with the other twelve. We will tell Nathaniel's story in the next chapter.

City and regional names like Scythia and Hieropolis do not mean anything to us today, however Phillip and Nathaniel were among the first to take the gospel to this area which is now known as Turkey. John

Zebedee's apocalypse or Revelation was written to the 7 churches of Asia. Phillip and his brother started these Churches. Phillip preached in the area known as Scythia for over 20 years starting churches and ordaining Pastors and Deacons. Phillip was said to have married a woman who traveled to France with him on his first missionary journey. They had twin daughters who are never named in history. Both Jerome and Isidore speak of these daughters so we know this was probably true. Legend tells us that these girls became powerful witnesses of Jesus and after their Mother died, continued to travel and minister with their Father Phillip. Many people do not like to acknowledge the marriages and families of the Apostles. This celibate tradition has been handed down for many years through many faiths and not just in the Catholic or Greek Orthodox traditions. I think we would like to raise these men to a higher level than just the average man, and then we are not expected to emulate their actions. I personally find a great deal of comfort in the fact that these men, while remarkable in devotion, were just like us with wives, families and friends.

After twenty years had passed, the pagan element of this city caught Phillip and tried to make him worship the god Mars. Phillip asked the people if they wanted to see who they were really worshiping and at that time, according to the old writings, a dragon appeared out of the statue. This dragon was bellowing fire and noxious fumes which were poisonous and many of the people began to fall ill and perish from the gases that came from this dragon. Phillip told them to break the statue and that would destroy the dragon and that they should receive Christ as their Savior from sin and no longer serve these idols.

The priests by this time had all been slain and the people were so afraid that they asked Phillip to send the dragon away. Phillip sent the dragon away as they asked and many of the people accepted Christ as savior and were healed and many thought to be dead stood up and listened to Phillips message and also were healed. This started a great revival in the area and many thousands came to Christ as a result of the testimony of these who were dead and now were alive! Phillip quoted his Master in his sermon: "I am the resurrection and the life, though you are dead, yet shall you live" This quote is found on many of the tombs of this city unto this day.

Phillip then went to the city of Hieropolis with his two daughters. There was a heresy arising among some who taught that Jesus did not have a human body, but that he had a heavenly body only which we could see and not touch. No one was more suited to put down this false doctrine better than Phillip. Having followed Jesus for three years, seeing him crucified and raised, Phillip knew exactly what Jesus looked like and saw his body bleed just like ours. By this time it was about AD 55 and Phillip knew that his time was soon at hand so he called the leaders of the churches to a meeting. He charged them to continue the ministry and to continue to plant the gospel in this land where he was called. A week later Phillip was taken by the same pagans who tried to make him worship Mars and was stoned though not yet dead and then crucified.

Phillip was known in the gospels as the one who saw the boy with the lunch, but said" It would take 200 days salary to buy enough bread to feed all these people." Andrew took the boy to Jesus anyway. Phillip seemed so practical. So like us when we look at what is possible. After the Resurrection, Phillip was transformed to a man who could feed the world with one loaf, the bread of life, Jesus. His ministry started the largest churches in the known world. His daughters never married according to legend, but were buried on his right and left side after many years of continued ministry.

Sandals in the Dust

Chapter VIII-Nathaniel Ben Tolomai (Bartholomew in Syrian)

Nathaniel Ben Tolomai is often better known as Bartholomew. This was his Syrian name, which means Son of God who holds the waters. Bar means son of and Tolomew means Son of God who holds back the waters. John Zebedee is the only Gospel writer who lists him by the name Nathaniel and since I am fond of John and this was his Aramaic name, I prefer it to the Syrian one.

Nathaniel and his brother Phillip or Philip were from Galilee, Cana to be more precise. They were herdsman and tanners by profession when called by the Master to follow them.

Philip was one of the disciples of John the Baptist who asked Jesus where he lived and Jesus replied: "Come and See." We fail to see the significance of this greeting because of our ignorance of the culture in those days. When Philip and John asked Jesus where he lived, He was supposed to have told them so they could stop by at a socially accepted hour on another day. For Jesus to basically reply come with me now was way out of the ordinary and would have been considered radical to invite people to come with Him to his home without notice for them to purchase the proper gifts customary to be given to the hosts when visitors arrived. Jesus was not interested in gifts, only in teaching them what they needed to know and to invite them to follow Him. Philip was so taken with this that he found his brother Nathaniel and told him about Jesus.

Nathaniel, who was well educated and knew the prophecies well, doubted that anything good could come from his own town or region. Philip used the new custom started by Jesus, who showed he was a fast learner, and replied to Nathaniel, "Come and See!" Of course we know that Jesus said of Nathaniel, "Behold an Israelite in whom is no guile!" Jesus knew the heart of Nathaniel and knew that Nathaniel did not believe that Jesus was the Messiah, but he soon changed his mind when Jesus told him that he had saw him under the tree earlier that day!

Nathaniel is not mentioned at all in the Gospels of Mathew, John Mark, Luke or John Zebedee again except to be listed as one of the twelve. The main reason for this is that many believe that a lost Gospel of Nathaniel or Bartholomew is still out there. There are many mentions of this throughout the old writings. Since the Gospels were written to compliment each other, if Nathaniel's Gospel story of Jesus had experiences that included him in them, naturally the other Gospel writers would have not included them in their own Gospels. Unless they were significant to main story of the Life, Death, Burial and Resurrection of Jesus, they would be no different than the different accounts of people and parables that are only found in one existing Gospel or another. John himself states that there were many other things Jesus did that he did not write down, so this is not in the realm of the impossible at all. Where is the Gospel of Nathaniel today? Only God knows where. Do not misunderstand me, I do believe that God has given us the Bible he wanted us to have.

Nathaniel preached the Gospel for some time in Ethiopia with Matthew. He copied his own copy of Matthew's Gospel to carry with him after he moved on. He then went to Asia Minor for a time with his brother Phillip, moved on to India with Thomas and finally ended up in the country of Armenia.

While in India, Nathaniel is supposed to have worked with Thomas to translate the first Gospel written in the Indian language of the time. He was there many years and learned the language and then taught Aramaic to an early convert and then read him the Gospel of Matthew. The man then translated the words back in his own language and in this way Nathaniel was able to make of Copy of the what we now call the Gospel of Matthew into the native language of the very people he was ministering to. This was a huge breakthrough into what we now consider just a standard practice of normal Missionary work.

The story of Nathaniel is recorded very completely in the Ante Nicene Fathers Volume VIII. The Next section will be based on this work.

Historians declare that India is divided into three parts; and the first is said to end at Ethiopia, and the second at Media, and the third completes the country; and the one portion of it ends in the dark, and the other in the ocean. To this India, then called Armenia, Nathaniel, the apostle of Christ went, and took up his quarters in the temple of Astaruth, and lived there as one of the pilgrims and the poor. In this temple, then, there was an idol called Astaruth, which was supposed to heal the infirm, but rather the more injured all. And the people were in entire ignorance of the true God; and from want of knowledge, but rather from the difficulty of going to any other, they all fled for refuge to the false god. And he brought upon them troubles, infirmities, damage, violence, and much affliction; and when any one sacrificed to him, the demon, retiring, appeared to give a cure to the person in trouble; and the foolish people, seeing this, believed in him. But the demons retired, not because they wished to cure men, but that they might the more assail them, and rather have them altogether in their power; and thinking that they were cured bodily, those that sacrificed to them were the more diseased in soul.

And it came to pass, that while the apostle of Christ, Nathaniel, stayed there, Astaruth gave no response, and was not able to heal. And when the temple was full of sick persons, who sacrificed to him daily, Astaruth could give no response; and sick persons who had come from far countries were lying there. When, therefore, in that temple not even one of the idols was able to give a response, and was of benefit neither to those that sacrificed to them nor to those who were in the agonies of death on their account, they were compelled to go to another city, where there was a temple of idols, where their great and most eminent god was called Bechur, having there sacrificed, they demanded, asking why their god Astaruth had not responded to them. And the demon Bechur answered and said to them: From the day and hour that the true God, who dwells in the heavens, sent his apostle Nathaniel into the regions here, your god Astaruth is held fast by chains of fire, and can no longer either speak or breathe. They said to him: And who is this Nathaniel? He answered: He is the friend of the Almighty God, and has just come into these parts, that he may take away all the worship of the idols in the name of his God. And the servants of the Greeks said to him: Tell us what he is like, that we may be able to find him.

And the demon answered and said: He has black hair, a shaggy head, a fair skin, large eyes, beautiful nostrils, his ears hidden by the hair of his head, with a yellow beard, a few gray hairs, of middle height, and neither tall nor stunted, but middling, clothed with a white undercoat bordered with purple, and upon his shoulders a very white cloak; and his clothes have been worn twenty-six years, but neither are they dirty, nor have they waxed old. Seven times a day he bends the knee to the Lord, and seven times a night does he pray to God. His voice is like the sonnet of a strong trumpet; there go along with him angels of God, who allow him neither to be weary, nor to hunger, nor to thirst; his face, and his soul, and his heart are always glad and rejoicing; he foresees everything, he knows and speaks every tongue of every nation. And behold now, as soon as you ask me, and I answer you about him, behold, he knows; for the angels of the Lord tell him; and if you wish to seek him, if he is willing he will appear to you; but if he shall not be willing, you will not be able to find him. I entreat you, therefore, if you shall find him, entreat him not to come here, lest his angels do to me as they have done to my brother Astaruth.

And when the demon had said this, he held his peace. And they returned, and set to work to look into every face of the pilgrims and poor men, and for two days they could find him nowhere. And it came to pass, that one who was a demoniac set to work to cry out: Apostle of the Lord, Nathaniel, thy prayers are burning me up. Then said the apostle to him: Hold thy peace, and come out of him. And that very hour, the man who had suffered from the demon for many years was set free.

And Polymius, the king of that country, happened to be standing opposite the apostle; and he had a daughter a demoniac, that is to say, a lunatic. And he heard about the demoniac that had been healed, and sent messengers to the apostle, saying: My daughter is grievously torn; I implore thee, therefore, as you have delivered him who suffered for many years, so also to order my daughter to be set free. And the apostle rose up, and went with them. And he sees the king's daughter bound with chains, for she used to tear in pieces all her limbs; and if any one came near her, she used to bite, and no one dared to come near her. The servants say to him: And who is it that dares to touch her? The apostle answered them: Loose her, and let her go. They say to him again: We have her in our power when she is bound with all our force, and dost thou bid us loose her? The apostle says to them: Behold, I keep her enemy bound, and are you even now afraid of her? Go and loose her; and when she has partaken of food, let her rest, and early to-morrow bring her to me. And they went and did as the apostle had commanded them; and thereafter the demon was not able to come near her.

Then the king loaded camels with gold and silver, precious stones, pearls, and clothing, and sought to see the apostle; and having made many efforts, and not found him, he brought everything back to his palace.

And it happened, when the night had passed, and the following day was dawning, the sun having risen, the apostle appeared alone with the king in his bed-chamber, and said to him: Why didst thou seek me yesterday the whole day with gold and silver, and precious stones, pearls, and raiment? For these gifts those persons long for who seek earthly things; but I seek nothing earthly, nothing carnal. Wherefore I wish to teach thee that God deigned to be born as a man out of a virgin's womb. He was conceived in the womb of the virgin; He took to Himself her who was always a virgin, having within herself Him who made the heaven and the earth, the sea, and all that therein is. He, born of a virgin, like mankind, took to Himself a beginning in time, He who has a beginning neither of times nor days; but He Himself made every beginning, and everything created, whether in things visible or invisible. Then the Son of God having been born of the virgin, and having become perfect man, and having been baptized, and after His baptism having fasted forty days, the tempter came and said to Him: If thou art the Son of God, tell these stones to become loaves. And He answered: Not on bread alone shall man live, but by every word of God. Thus therefore the devil, which through eating bad conquered the first man, was conquered through the fasting of the second man; and as he through want of self-restraint had conquered the first man, the son of the virgin earth, so we shall conquer through the fasting of the second Adam, the Son of the Virgin Mary.

The king says to him: And how is it that you said just now that she was the first virgin of whom was born God and man? And the apostle answered: I give thanks to the Lord that you hear me gladly. The first man, then, was called Adam; he was formed out of the earth. And the earth, his mother out of which he was, was virgin, because it had neither been polluted by the blood of man nor opened for the burial of any one. The earth, then, was like the virgin, in order that Sin, who conquered the son of the virgin Earth, might be conquered by the Son of the Virgin Mary. And, behold, Sin did conquer; for his wicked craft, through the eating of the tree by which man, being deceived, came forth from paradise, kept paradise shut. Thereafter this Son of the virgin conquered all the craft of the devil. And his craft was such, that when he saw the Son of the virgin fasting forty days, he knew in truth that He was the true God. The true God and man, therefore, hath not given Himself out to be known, except to those who are pure in heart, and who serve Him by good works. The devil himself, therefore, when he saw that after the forty days He was again hungry, was deceived into thinking that He was not God, and said to Him, Why have you been hungry? Tell these stones to become loaves, and eat. And the Lord answered him, Listen, devil; although you may lord it over man, because he has not kept the commandment of God. I have fulfilled the righteousness of God in having fasted, and shall destroy your power, so that you shall no longer lord it over man. And when he saw himself conquered, he again takes Jesus to an exceeding high mountain, and shows Him all the kingdoms of the world, and says, All these will I give thee, if you will fall down and worship me. The Lord says to him, Get thee behind me, Satan; for it is written, Thou shall worship the Lord thy God, and Him only shall thou serve. And there was a third temptation for the Lord; for he takes Him up to the pinnacle of the temple, and says, if thou art the Son of God, cast thyself down. The Lord says to him, Thou shall not tempt the Lord thy God. And the devil disappeared. And he indeed that once conquered Adam, the son of the virgin earth, was thrice conquered by Christ, the Son of the Virgin Mary.

And when the Lord had conquered the tyrant called Sin or Death, He sent His apostles into the entire world, that He might redeem His people from the deception of the devil; and one of these I am, an apostle of Christ. On this account we seek not after gold and silver, but rather despise them, because we labor to be rich in that place where the kingdom of Him alone endures for ever.

Wherefore also the demon sitting in your temple, which makes responses to you, is kept in chains through the angel of the Lord who has sent me. Because if thou shall believe and be baptized, and wishes thyself to be enlightened, I will make thee behold Him, and learn from how great evils thou hast been redeemed. At the same time hear also by what means he injures all those who are lying sick in the temple. The devil himself by his own art causes the men to be sick, and again to be healed, in order that they may the more believe in the idols, and in order that he may have place the more in their souls, in order that they may say to the stock and the stone, Thou art our God. But that demon that dwells in the idol is held in subjection, conquered by me, and is able to give no response to those who sacrifice and pray there. And if thou wish to prove that it is so, I order him to return into the idol, and I will make him confess with his own mouth that he is bound, and able to give no response.

The apostle says to him: Why dost thou not save all that have come to thee? The demon says to him: When we injure their bodies, unless we first injure their souls, we do not let their bodies go. The apostle says to him: And how do you injure their souls? The demon answered him: When they believe that we are gods, and sacrifice to us, God withdraws his Spirit from those who sacrifice, and we do not take away the sufferings of their bodies, but retire into their souls.

Then the apostle says to the people: Behold, the god whom you thought to cure you, does the more mischief to your souls and bodies. Hear even now your Maker who dwells in the heavens, and do not believe in lifeless stones and stocks. And if you wish that I should pray for you, and that all these may receive health, take down this idol, and break it to pieces; and when you have done this, I will sanctify this temple in the name of our Lord Jesus Christ; and all who believe I will baptize in the baptism of the Lord.

Then the king gave orders and all the people brought ropes and crowbars, and were not at all slow to take down the idol. Then the apostle says to them: Unfasten the ropes. And when they had unfastened them, he said to the demon dwelling in it: In the name of our Lord Jesus Christ, come out of this idol, and go into a desert place, where neither winged creature utters a cry, nor voice of man has ever been heard. And straightway he arose at the word of the apostle, and lifted it up from its foundations; and in that same hour all the idols that were in that place were broken to pieces.

Then all cried out with one voice, saying: He alone is God Almighty whom Nathaniel the apostle proclaims. Then the king, and also the queen, with their two sons, and with all his people, and with all the multitude of the city, and every city round about, and country, and whatever land his kingdom ruled over, were saved, and believed, and were baptized in the name of the Father, and the Son, and the Holy Spirit. And the king laid aside his diadem, and followed Nathaniel, the apostle of Christ.

And after these things the unbelievers of the Greeks, having come together to Astreges the king, who was the elder brother of the king who had been baptized, say to him: O king, thy brother Polymius has become disciple to a certain magician, who has taken down our temples, and broken our gods to pieces. And while they were thus speaking and weeping, behold, again there came also some others from the cities round about, both priests and people; and they set about weeping and making accusations before the king. Then King Astreges in a rage sent a thousand armed men along with those priests, in order that, wherever they should find the apostle, they might bring him to him bound. And when they had done so, and found him, and brought him, he says to him: Art thou he who has perverted my brother from the gods? To whom the apostle answered: I have not perverted him, but have converted him to God. The king says to him: Art thou he who caused our gods to be broken in pieces? The apostle says to him: I gave power to the demons that were in them, and they broke in pieces the dumb and senseless idols, that all men might believe in God Almighty, who dwells in the heavens. The king says to him: As thou hast made my brother deny his gods, and believe in thy God, so I also will make you reject thy God and believe in my gods. The apostle says to him: If I have bound and kept in subjection the god which thy brother worshipped, and at my order the idols were broken in pieces, if thou also art able to do the same to my God, thou canst persuade me also to sacrifice to thy gods; but if thou canst do nothing to my God, I will break all thy gods in pieces; but do thou believe in my God. And when he had thus spoken, the king was informed that this god Baldad and all the other idols had fallen down, and were broken in pieces. Then the king rent the purple in which he was clothed, and ordered the apostle Nathaniel to be beaten with rods; and after to be flayed alive and to be beheaded.

And innumerable multitudes came from all the cities, to the number of twelve thousand, who had believed in him along with the king; and they took up the remains of the apostle with singing of praise and with all glory, and they laid them in the royal tomb, and glorified God. And the king Astreges having heard of this, ordered him to be thrown into the sea; and his remains were carried into the island of Liparis.

And it came to pass on the thirtieth day after the apostle was carried away, that the king Astreges was overpowered by a demon and miserably strangled;

and all the priests were strangled by demons, and perished on account of their rising against the apostle, and thus died by an evil fate.

And there was great fear and trembling, and all came to the Lord, and were baptized by the presbyters who had been ordained by the apostle Nathaniel. And according to the commandment of the apostle, all the clergy of the people made King Polymius Pastor; and in the name of our Lord Jesus Christ he received the grace of healing, and began to do signs. And he remained Pastor for twenty years; and having prospered in all things, and governed the church well, and guided it in right opinions, he fell asleep in peace.

Ancient Flaying knife like that one used on Nathaniel

Sandals in the Dust

MATTHEW BEN LEVI

Matthew Ben Levi is the Ninth Apostle written about in this book. Matthew or Levi as some call him was the brother of Thomas and was raised by Levi in a very strict sect. Thomas and Matthew were by far the most educated of the original 12 and while Thomas was raised at the feet of Gamaliel the great Jewish teacher, Matthew was chosen by the family to become the local tax collector.

Many people have misunderstood the role of a tax collector in this society. Most of them came from the tribe of Levi for the people were accustomed to priests collecting their money for offerings at the temple. The Romans understood this and used this advantage for their own purposes. The Tax collector would be given a bill of taxes to collect and to make a living; he would have to charge a fee for taxes collected. In other words, the Romans had a system that made a thief out of the Publican or Tax Collector. The Tax collector could not tell the people what was being done or he would be killed either by the Romans or by the people themselves. It was out of this corrupt system that Matthew was rescued that day when Jesus asked him to follow him. It is no wonder that he immediately left his receipts and followed Jesus.

The story of Zacchaeus in Luke 19 is brought to a whole new light with this knowledge. Zacchaeus was the chief of all Tax Collectors and no doubt had been told of Matthew's desertion of his duties to follow Christ. He was amazed that a "holy prophet" would allow a tax collector to follow and be numbered as a disciple. That is why he inquired so much about this Jesus and wanted to see Him and maybe during this research he realized his own sin. In this way when Jesus called Matthew, he prepared the way for the conversion of Zacchaeus.

Matthew was a very gifted follower. He spoke several languages including Aramaic, Hebrew, Latin, Greek and some parts of the original Gospel of Matthew are written in the language of the ancient Chaldeans. Matthew's first mission trip was to the county of Ethiopia. He stayed in the home of the Eunuch of the Candace or Queen of Ethiopia, who was converted by the deacon Phillip as mentioned in the book of Acts. Even the Eunuch was amazed at Matthew's gift of languages. He asked him how he was able to communicate in so many languages and Matthew replied that even though he was well taught in seven or eight languages, that ever since the day of Pentecost, he was able to use any language needed to share the Gospel with anyone by help of the Holy Spirit. He called this the gift of tongues, available to all believers. Today many people think of the gift of tongues as a gift of unknown languages, but in all of my research of the 12, each time this gift was manifest, it was in known languages to expedite the sharing of the Gospel.

Many have wondered why the Apostles traveled to take the Gospel to remote random places. There was nothing random about the choices they made. There were tribes of the Northern Kingdom of Israel scattered throughout all of these places. Ethiopia as we know today had a large population of the old tribe of Dan. Many of these people today have returned to Israel and even serve in the Israeli Army. There are cults in the U.S. that say that they are descendents of this tribe, but unless they are from Ethiopia, this is highly unlikely. Matthew began his mission much as a modern missionary would begin today. He had a base of operations at an existing believer's home and then reached out from there to the surrounding areas and peoples. Now we will talk about the conversions of believers in Ethiopia and the martyrdom of this very special Apostle.

Matthew Ben Levi was called to confront what the local people of Ethiopia called Dragons. They were in fact very large evil spirits or demons. Matthew confronted them and in the name of Jesus put them both to sleep. A very large crowd gathered and the Apostle taught them about the Earthly Paradise from which God drove Adam and Eve because of Sin. He then taught them about the Heavenly Paradise that we all can attain through faith in Christ. As he was preaching to a crowd of several thousand, there arose a disturbance from the palace, which spread, to the whole crowd. The Crown Prince of Ethiopia had been ill and had suddenly died. The palace advisors told the King that the prince had joined the gods and that the King should build a mighty temple to his son for worship. The Eunuch who was converted in the book of Acts put these advisors in prison and summoned the Apostle. With great crowds watching Matthew prayed and asked God to raise the prince to life. The Prince suddenly stood up and was not ill anymore. The King sent heralds throughout the Kingdom telling everyone to come see the "god-man." Matthew went to the King and told him that he was not God and then shared the whole story of Jesus with him. The entire royal family of Ethiopia was converted and the King asked Matthew what he could do. Matthew asked him to build a great place of worship so that all could hear of the Love of God and the sacrifice of Jesus on the Cross.

Matthew transcribed in Hebrew the Logia (Greek-collection) apparently an early Aramaic collection of the sayings of Christ. The Hebrew is believed by many to have been written about 38 AD. The traditional date is 37 AD. The Apostle Matthew aided his memory by writing down Jesus' sayings in Aramaic. The Aramaic original was composed around then or later and the Greek gospel about 60AD. Many copies of Matthew's collection were quickly made and distributed among the churches in Palestine. Translations into the Greek were also widely circulated. Papias says that Matthew "put together the oracles of the Lord in the Hebrew language, and each one interpreted them as best he could." Not our present gospel of Matthew, but the collection of sayings. This first collection to appear was called "Matthew's Sayings of Jesus". Then Mark's gospel came, then the gospel of Matthew, combining both.

After the Church was finished Matthew was the Pastor for over thirty years. He is believed to have preached the gospel in Africa, to the south of the

Caspian Sea, Persia, the kingdom of the Parthians, Macedonia and Syria. .

He evangelized much of the land of Ethiopia and Egypt, his followers founding the first church in Alexandria. The daughter of the King of Naddaber became a very devout follower of God. Even though she was very beautiful, she would not allow herself to be given in marriage because of her love of God. There are some, who would call her the first Nun, but according to scripture, the Apostle Paul tells us that it is better to be single and serve God, but if you have problems with lust, then it is better to be married than to burn. There is no scriptural precedent for being a celibate, the practice not becoming mandate for Catholic clergy until about the 3rd or 4th Centuries. It is said that the King's brother-in law wanted the princess as his wife but she would not even look at him. Matthew is said to have told the man to stay away from her. In a burning rage of lust and jealousy he sent soldiers to put Matthew in prison. Matthew was rescued from prison by one of his fellow

Apostles, Andrew and healed of the wounds he had received from the soldiers. Andrew converted many to Christ in this village and then departed. Matthew went back to his Church and when the King's brother-in-law heard that he was free he came to the Church with his guard and had them kill Matthew while he was kneeling in prayer. He was stabbed in the back by a sword and then according to some legends, nailed to the cross in the church itself. Matthew was obedient to God until the last of his days and each year as the time of Christmas approaches I remember that much of what I know of Christ came from the words and works of Matthew, and that besides my salvation is the greatest gift of all.

Sandals in the Dust

Chapter X-Matthias Ben Judah

MATTHIAS BEN JUDAH

Matthias Ben Judah is the last of the Apostles mentioned in the scriptures other than the Apostle Paul. He is not mentioned at all in the gospels. As I have said in the first chapter of this book, he was chosen to the replacement of Judas Iscariot who hung himself after betraying the master. He was chosen by holy lot, which was the same way the priests of the Old Testament would determine God's will. The Urim and the Thumin were stones, black on one side and white on the other. When the priests could not determine God's will or a guilt or innocence of someone, they would go in front of the veil just outside of the "Holy of Holies," and cast the lots prayerfully. Two white stones meant yes or innocent. Two blacks meant guilty and a black and white combination meant acquittal or there is not definitive answer. Whether or not the Apostles actually used real lots or just prayed significantly and trusted the God to guide them, we will never know for sure. This one thing is for sure, Barsabas or Joseph the Just was a brother of three of the Apostles, James, Jude and Simon Alpheus. Barsabas was also a first Cousin of

James and John. You would think that he had the inside track if this had been a popularity or fleshly contest. How surprised Matthias must have been when the lot fell on him? This is his story, a story of Christmas Time from Bethlehem of Judea:

Matthias was from a poor family of Shepherds in the hillsides of Judea around the city of Bethlehem. One of his many jobs each day was to take the night watch with the dogs and make sure that the sheep were safe. He would have kept to himself most of the time, not going into the city unless sent on an errand from his family. From the book of Matthew we read about the story of Joseph and Mary, how there was no room at the inn and that they were given shelter for her upcoming birth in a cave or stable that was behind the Inn. One night as Matthias was keeping watch, the air was suddenly filled with heavenly beings. They told him not to be afraid, but to go and find the babe wrapped in swaddling or grave wrappings. They said the baby would be lying in a manger. Matthias and his family went to the stable guided by a light that had appeared. The light seemed to shine upon a cave on the edge of the city. Inside they found Mary, Joseph and the baby Jesus. Matthias was but a child but the words of the Angels had a strange effect on him. He wanted to serve the new King in any way he could so he took off his outer cloak and told Mary that she could use it for a blanket to keep the new King warm.

Matthias gives his blanket to the Baby Jesus

Over the next few weeks, Matthias was constantly visiting the home of his new King. Joseph had obtained work as a carpenter to pay his taxes. Mary was alone each day with the new baby. Matthias brought food and anything else he could find to help his new friends. After almost two years had passed by one night Matthias saw a large caravan coming in the night from the direction of Jerusalem. The men were strangely dressed and asked him where they could find the new King that was born. Matthias knew exactly which King they were talking about and led them to the house of Mary and Joseph. The Gospels tell us that when they came unto the house that worshiped the child and gave gifts of Gold, Frankincense and Myrrh. After they left that night Matthias went back to his sheep very happy. Now he was not the only one to worship the new King. How sad and surprised he was when Mary and Joseph came to him that night as they were leaving. They thanked him for his help and the little baby Jesus kissed Matthias and said a simple goodbye in the

Aramaic. Matthias cried himself to sleep that night and decided that he would wait for them to come back.

What a terrible day followed when Herod's soldiers came into town and killed every baby that was two years old or younger. Matthias now knew why his King had left him. God had saved him from the wrath of Herod.

Almost 10 years passes and Herod the King finally dies. Matthias was with his sheep one night when an Angel told him to go to the Land of Egypt and seek out the family of Joseph and Mary with the young Child. Matthias now about 18 years of age does as the Angel has requested. Jesus is now about the age of 11 or almost 12. According to legend, after Joseph was told in a dream to return to Israel that he was planning on going back to Bethlehem. Matthias told him that Archelias the son of Herod still knew of his father's obsession with the King he tried to kill almost 10 years ago and told them to go to where Mary's

family was in Galilee. Joseph had prospered as a
Carpenter in Egypt and had plenty of money for the
travel. Part of the Journey was by barge or boat up
the Nile River.

Rich Mullins, the famous Christian singer/songwriter
had an untimely death several years ago, but had
written a song about Jesus in Africa and Egypt that
was on his last Demo. Whenever I hear this song I
like to think of Matthias riding the boat up the Nile
and thinking that his Deliverer was returning to
Israel!

Joseph took his wife and her child, and they went to Africa
To escape the rage of a deadly king
There along the banks of the Nile, Jesus listened to the song
That the captive children used to sing
They were singing'
My Deliverer is coming - my Deliverer is standing by
My Deliverer is coming - my Deliverer is standing by
He will never break His promise - He has written it upon
the sky
My Deliverer is coming - my Deliverer is standing by

Through a dry and thirsty land, water from the Kenyon
heights
Pours itself out of Lake Sangra's broken heart
There in the Sahara winds Jesus heard the whole world cry
For the healing that would flow from His own scars
The world was singing
My Deliverer is coming - my Deliverer is standing by
My Deliverer is coming - my Deliverer is standing by
I will never doubt His promise though I doubt my heart, I
doubt my eyes
My Deliverer is coming - my Deliverer is standing
My Deliverer is coming - my Deliverer is standing by
He will never break His promise though the stars should
break faith with the sky
My Deliverer is coming - my Deliverer is standing by

Clement of Alexandria, *Stromata* 7.13.82.1 has written that they say that Matthias the apostle in the *Traditions* says at every opportunity, "If the neighbor of an elect person dies in his sin, the elect person sins. For if he had led himself as the word dictates, the neighbor would have been in awe of his life so that he would receive the Christ."

This was one of 5 fragments that survive of the
Gospel of Matthias. Note how important the
testimony to a neighbor was to Matthias. This is the
true heart of a missionary. There is a trend in modern
times to go on a "Mission Trip." How many of us
will travel to a far away land to witness, but never tell
our neighbor across the street of his need for a Savior.
Matthias was chosen to take the Gospel to the very
hillsides where he was once a shepherd. In Judea
Matthias preached for many years. It is said that
many were won to Christ because of the testimony of
the Birth of Christ after which Matthias could calmly
say: "I was there at the Stable, I saw and heard the
Angels. I led the Wise Men to the House who had
followed the star." Matthias was a witness to the
entire story of Jesus like no other and his testimony is
included in Matthew and Luke's Gospels. Tradition
also tells us that Matthias traveled later in life to
Macedonia and even to what is modern Germany
with the Gospel. Once he was given a cup of wine to
drink that had been laced with a poison that would

cause blindness. Matthias was not harmed by the poison and healed the blindness of over 250 persons who had already drunk the poison in the last year. Tradition tells us that after preaching in the city of Trier Germany, that he was captured by agents of the High Priests and dragged back to Jerusalem in chains. He was later crucified and died about 68AD. His body was taken to Rome in the third century and later brought back to the city of Trier by Constantine.

Tomb of Matthias

About 15 years ago I was privileged to travel to the city of Trier to see the Church and Tomb of Matthias. I was just beginning a serious study of the Apostles at this time. I had already seen the statue of Paul looking down on the twin cities of Buda and Pest, in Hungary. I had also seen the site of the famous thorn tree of Joseph of Arimathea in Southern England. Nothing had prepared me for the site of the actual body of one the Apostles. Here in this Beautiful church, settled in this storybook little village was the actual body seen through the glass, one whom had witnessed the birth, ministry, death and resurrection of our Lord. Matthias lived his life as a testimony that the people next door are as important to God as the people halfway around the world. I think Matthias would have liked the words to the song sung by Steven Curtis Chapman:

Imagine this...I get a phone call from Regis
He says, "Do you want to be a millionaire?"
They put me on the show and I win with two lifelines to
spare
Now picture this...I act like nothing ever happened
And bury all the money in a coffee can
Well, I've been given more than Regis ever gave away
I was a dead man who was called to come out of my grave

And I think it's time for makin' some noise
Wake the neighbors, get the word out
Come on...crank up the music...climb a mountain and
shout
This is life we've been given made to be lived out
So la la la la live out loud

Sandals in the Dust

Chapter XI-Who was Judas Iscariot

Judas after the betrayal of Jesus

After telling you the background of Matthias I thought it would be important for you to understand exactly whom it was that Matthias Replaced. Judas Iscariot is synonymous with the English word Traitor. There are two different versions of why Judas betrayed Christ. One is that he was a thief as it says in the Gospels. That he was so disgusted with the waste of the ointment which could have sold for 300 pence that he agreed to discern Jesus from James the son of Alpheus, who looked so much like Jesus, for 30 "ten- pence" pieces of silver which was 300 pence. In the famous movie "King of Kings" Judas is a friend of the Simon the Zealot and feels that when Jesus is threatened by the Romans, that He would have no choice but to show his real power and that then could be made King. While there is some truth in both schools of thought, there is definitely more scripture to back up the first theory. After I relate the written accounts of Judas' background, I will let you decide for yourself.

There was a man named Simon who lived in Jerusalem. He was of the tribe of Dan. His wife was named Ciborea. One night while they were sleeping Ciborea awoke and told her husband that she had a terrible dream: That they had conceived that night a child who would be a shame to all people. Simon told her that was nonsense and she warned him that if they had a child nine months hence, that he would know that she was right and that they must do something about it. Sure enough nine months to the day Ciborea bore a son. Simon and Ciborea were so anguished over the dream she had that they decided to tell everyone that the child was stillborn. They put the child in a basket and placed it in the Mediterranean Sea.

The basket drifted to the Island known as Iscariot, hence the name given to Judas. The Queen of this land found the basket and took the child home secretly and told everyone that this was her son. The Queen soon had another son and Judas as he was called by now, began to treat the royal heir badly.

The Queen soon confessed her folly to the King and
the young boy was told the truth. On his 18th
birthday he slew the son of the King with his bare
hands and made his way to Jerusalem. While in
Jerusalem he became a confidant of Herod and later
Pontius Pilate. One day he was in a field that was
owned by his real father and got into an argument
with him. His father, Simon, did not know who Judas
was and he struck him. Judas struck back and killed
his own father. Witnesses bore out that Simon had
indeed struck first so Pontius Pilate decreed that
Judas should inherit the land and take the widow to
be his wife! The wedding night when Judas came in
to Ciborea, she was weeping and began to tell how
God was punishing her for killing her son. Judas
heard enough of her story and then told his. Low and
behold he realized that he had married his own
Mother. Judas wanted to do something to show God
how sorry he was so he went to the Temple and sat
with Thomas and others at the feet of Gamaliel.
When Thomas began to follow Jesus, Judas did so as
well and Jesus made him the keeper of all funds that

were taken in from people. The scriptures tell us that Judas was a thief and that he stole even from our Lord. Now we come to the two versions of the betrayal, which I have already recounted above. Judas then upon reflection of his actions to Christ and other terrible things he had done hung himself and the bible says that the tree limb broke and that his bowels spilled out upon the ground.

Like Cain, he slew the only brother he had ever known, like Nimrod, he killed his own father and married his mother. The only question is why Jesus would ever allow someone like this to follow him. Maybe only someone this wicked could have betrayed our Lord or maybe, just maybe, like the parable when Jesus asks who will love him more and the answer is the one who was forgiven the most.

Since all sin bears the penalty of death, does it matter which ones we have committed. If a court of Law convicts us of speeding, can we use the defense, hey, it was not like I killed anyone or are we still guilty.

The scripture tells us in James chapter two that if we keep the whole law but offend only in one part, we are guilty of all. Judas had a choice of Mercy and forgiveness and he chose death and hell.

Sandals in the Dust

Chapter XII-Thomas Ben Levi

Thomas Ben Levi is the 11th Apostle in our journey. Thomas is most famous in the scriptures for his doubt, not his faith. Thomas was the brother of Matthew and was raised in the tradition of the Levi or Cohen priests. While Matthew was taught the business of the tax collector, Thomas was schooled at the Temple in Jerusalem under the teachings of Nicodemus and Gamaliel. Tradition tells us that Thomas first met the master when Nicodemus came to Jesus by night. Thomas is thought to have been the very pragmatic Apostle, for example when Jesus said he was going to Jerusalem, Thomas said, "Come let us go that we may die with him." In fact, when Thomas became a believer after Jesus appeared to him and invited him to touch his hands and feet, Thomas became one of the greatest Missionaries aside from Paul in the first Century.

According to the INDIAN TRADITION, Thomas came by sea, first landed at Cranganore about the year AD 52; converted high cast Hindu families in Cranganore, Palayur, Quilon and some other places, visited the Coromandel Coast, making conversions, crossed over to China and preached the Gospel. Returning to India he organized the Christians of Malabar under some Pastors from among the leading families he had converted and erected few public places of worship.

Thomas then moved to the Coromandel and suffered martyrdom on or near the Little Mount. His body was brought to the town of Mylapore and was buried in the shrine built for him there. In support of the early Christianization of North India we do not possess any actual vestiges as we do for South India.

The South India claim to the apostolate of Thomas is supported by two monuments: THE COMMUNITY OF ST. THOMAS CHRISTIANS with their living tradition and the tomb of Mylapore which is definitely identified as the burial place of Thomas at least from the 14th century onwards.

These considerations have forced a number of scholars to postulate an argument of convergence in favor of the following conclusion: THOMAS the Apostle preached the Gospel in South India and the origin of INDIAN CHRISTIANS at least initially, is to be attributed to this preaching.

Apostle Thomas was martyred in Mylapore near Madras. (Tradition calls this place Kalloor - the place of rock) in Tamilnadu State, India. The traditional date of martyrdom is 19th of December, 72 AD. His followers took his body and buried him in the tombs of the Chiefs. A merchant from Edessa in Turkey who visited that region exhumed his body and took it to Turkey where it was entombed in about AD 200. We can still see these tombs in Mylapore and in Edessa.

When the rich young ruler wanted to follow Jesus he said that he had kept all of the commandments from his youth. Jesus then told him to give all his money and possessions to the poor so that he would have treasure in heaven and then come and follow Him.

The man went away sorrowful because he was very rich and did not want to give it all away. Jesus then told the Apostles that it was easier for a Camel to enter the eye of the needle than for a rich man to enter heaven. Jesus was talking about the needle gate of Jerusalem that was so low to the ground that unless a camel was lowered to its knees first the front, then the back, he was too high up to fit into the gate. One of the Apostles asked who then could be saved. Jesus told them that nothing was impossible with God. This example must have played a strong role in shaping the character of Thomas, as you will see in the next story.

Thomas had returned to India after a missionary journey into China and men named Abannes approached him and said that he was looking for someone to design and build a palace or mansion for the King of India. Thomas told him that he could do this for the King and he accompanied Abannes to the court of Indian Royalty. There the King told Thomas exactly what he wanted and where he wanted it built.

Then he gave a huge fortune of money and materials to Thomas and told him that much more was at his disposal and that he had two years to complete the task. The King then traveled to the other side of India to await his new palace. During the two years of the Kings absence Thomas used the money he left to feed the poor, to house the orphan, to support the widows and since he done it all in the Kings name, the King became almost a saint in the eyes of the people. Thomas preached the Gospel in the city and healed the sick and was equally a favorite of all. During this time the Kings Brother-in Law was sick and he died. The King returned with the body for burial. Thomas met them as they came and prayed and asks God to rise up the brother of the King. When the Kings brother was alive he immediately began to tell the King of a beautiful city where a great Mansion had been prepared with the Kings name on it, but unless the King denounced his false gods and received Christ as his savior, he would never live in it. The King told him to be silent, as he would soon live in his own new Palace. That's when he arrived in the town of Mylapore and saw that there was no new Palace. Thomas told him that his brother spoke the truth, that he had followed the example of Jesus and given away the riches to the poor that the King could have a Palace or Mansion in Heaven. The King was enraged and sent Thomas to the Prison.

Over the next few weeks the King tried to execute Thomas many ways, through red-hot irons; water came from the ground and cooled them. By throwing him into a fiery pit, the fire went out and he emerged unharmed. Thomas kept preaching to his family and many of them had by now become believers. The King then decided that if he placed Thomas in the temple of his gods, that he would make his own God angry and then maybe God would kill him. When Thomas stood before the Idols, they immediately began to melt. The King then knew that the God of Thomas was the only God and at that moment he too became a believer. The high priest of the pagan gods became so angry that he immediately raised a sword high and plunged it into Thomas so that Thomas died on the 19th of December, 72 AD. The place was called Little Mount or the place of the rock.

The Doubting Thomas-India

On the Malabar Coast of India today, one of the only remaining Christian movements is called the Disciples of Thomas. Just like when Thomas saw Jesus arisen and said "My Lord and my God!" These Christians still start each prayer with the same phrase almost 2000 years later. There are many Tombs and Churches left by the Apostles in many lands, but this real life example in India is perhaps the greatest Christian legacy left to us in modern times. In my mind I can see a street of Gold in the Kingdom of Heaven, with many beautiful houses. I would like to think that the King of India and Thomas visit each other often in that city with no death, no artificial lights and certainly no locks on the doors.

Sandals in the Dust

Part XIII-John Ben Zebedee

The Beloved Apostle John Ben Zebedee:

My Little Children, as I approach the 97th year of life on this earth, I wanted the World to know the whole story. What really happened to us after our Lord ascended into heaven? After Jesus was gone, we were left to tell His story to the World. We did. We took the Gospel to Africa, Cathay (Asia), and to the Western Shores. (Europe) We told his story to the peoples of every known language and culture. We wrote accounts of our Lord's Birth, Ministry, Death and Resurrection and have established Churches and Shepherds every place that our foot touched the ground. We laid the foundation for centuries to come. But now that I alone am left, I recall Brother Simon's question to our Lord, "What shall this man do?" I have decided that our story will be an example, a lesson even to all that read it. I will tell of the footprints of the twelve. **Footprints fade quickly in the Dust. You must follow while there is still light.** *I am the only one who can tell this story, my beloved, as I am the Last of the Apostles. (John the Beloved, Excerpt from "The Last of the Apostles")*

The Paragraph above is from my book, which is a work of fiction. If only we had a scroll to tell us all the things that I have spent the last 40 years of my life researching.

The story of the Apostle John is a love story of a small boy whose older cousin, Jesus, became his hero. John would understand best that to enter the Kingdom of Heaven, you must come as a child, for when John was born, Jesus was already about 18 years of age. John was the youngest son of Zebedee and Miriam or Mary and was brother to James. From the time John could walk he was learning to be a fisherman. But John was also learning other things. There is a story of how one day when left behind by the other fisherman, John, who was only 6 or 7, was angry and wanted to prove that he too could catch fish. He took a net and cast it out into the sea and sat out all night. Of course, next to the shore, John was not likely to catch more than just a couple of small fish. As the ships where returning to shore and still about 100 yards away, Jesus who was in His twenties, walked by on his way to a job He was doing for his step-father Joseph, he simply looked at John and smiled. Suddenly John's net began to fill with hundreds of Fishes. Simon Peter and Andrew were amazed that such a small boy could catch so many fish! John's catch actually out-numbered that of both boats. Note that later when Jesus began his ministry, Peter was astounded by a huge catch of fish, whereas James seemed to take in all in stride. I believe that Peter suddenly recalled this incident and realized that it had been Jesus all along.

After this, John was said to have spent much of his boyhood talking to Jesus or his Cousin John (later called John the Baptist.) Once John came to Jesus upset because he had been using a favorite basket of his mothers at the Sea, the tide had come in and taken it. Jesus walked to the Sea and asked John where it had gone and John pointed to a small dot floating on the waves far out to Sea by now. Jesus walked out to the basket, picked it up, and then carried it back to John. Jesus held a finger to His lips and walked away. John never told about the basket until late in his life as a Pastor in the great city of Ephesus which is in Modern Turkey today.

John first began to search for God's will in his life by following John the Baptist. John's mother and Jesus' mother were sisters. John the Baptist was a second cousin of Jesus which would make the Apostle John a cousin of John the Baptist as well. John would take them to the river Jordan and would preach about the coming Kingdom of God and then Baptize or purify the believers in his message there in the Jordan itself. John was there the day that his other cousin, Jesus showed up to be baptized. He witnessed the Holy Spirit coming down like a dove and Heard the audible voice of the Father saying: "This is my beloved Son in whom I am well pleased!" This was the first example of God the Father, the Son and the Holy Spirit all present at the same time. John and Andrew heard John the Baptist say of Jesus, "Behold the Lamb of God who takes away the Sins of the World!" John and Andrew became the first to follow Jesus. Jesus said: "The first shall be last and the last first." John was the first of the Apostles to Follow and believe in whom Jesus is and was the last of the Apostles left here to minister to the Church.

There are several incidents in the Gospels about John that can be very misunderstood. You have to understand that John was about 13 when he followed Jesus, by far the youngest of the Apostles, and that he was a first cousin of Jesus. When John describes himself as the "Disciple whom Jesus loved" it can be very misunderstood unless you know that John is 13 by many still considered a boy. When in the upper room, John is leaning on Jesus and Peter uses John to get information about the betrayer, again, the age and relationship make it seem clear. Apart from Matthias, who also knew Jesus as a child, John was the only other Apostle who could see Jesus very clearly for who He was. When Jesus was being led to trial, John walks in boldly with no fear of arrest, how could this youth be threatening to the guards, where as Peter feels the need to mask his appearance. When Mary came with news of the resurrection, John out runs

Peter to the Tomb, but being young, he stays outside of the tomb, whereas Peter just goes in. John immediately believed, but Peter, being a rational adult, took a little more time and evidence to believe

After the Resurrection, John was beaten with Peter and was present during the miracle of the man who was begging for Silver and started "Walking and Leaping and Praising God!" John's role becomes unclear, as he was probably considered too young to take a leadership role. Eventually John took the Gospel to Ephesus and from a small group of believers and with the help of Clement, a disciple of Peter, started what was to become one of greatest and largest churches in the first Century. By 80 AD, only John and possible Simon Alpheus remained. Simon Alpheus lived the longest life of any of the Apostles, but John was much younger and lived well into the second Century. John became quite a subject of persecution when he was the Last of the Apostles. Domitian was then the Emperor of Rome. Rome was the capitol city a large nation from Italy that at that time ruled much of the known world. This nation was known as the Roman Empire. The Emperor summoned John to Rome in chains and under armed guard. There he had John placed in a cauldron of boiling oil. When John did not suffer harm he was embarrassed and gave him an audience before his throne. While there he gave join a goblet of new wine that was laced with the deadliest of poison. John drank it down with no ill effects. The emperor was now so embarrassed that he could not kill the frail old man that he ordered him to exile on an Island called Patmos. Exile was like marooning or stranding John on an Island where he would be all alone. The Emperor did not understand that someone like John was never alone.

While on this Island John received his Revelation from Jesus about the end of days and a message for the seven churches in Asia. This work called The Revelation of John is one of the most misunderstood and debated books in the entire Bible. Today many believe that this book has already happened in history, but others, like me, believe that these things have yet to happen. Knowing the simple and loving matter in which John communicated to others all of his life, I find it hard to believe that he would not want us to read and believe this book as simply as possible. This book gives us many glimpses of Heaven for the first time.

After the death of Domitian, John was allowed to leave Patmos and return to Ephesus. By this time he was over 99 years old and was very frail and could not walk. His disciples carried him in a chair to Church and even though he could not move his mouth well, the great historian Jerome tells us that he repeated the Phrase "Little Children, Love one another" with each step.

By this time John's fame as a preacher, Apostle, Missionary and Writer was spread throughout the known world. People would travel hundreds of miles to attend Church in Ephesus so that they could see John and many would bring the sick for healing up unto the day of his death.

In our modern times this kind of fame does not really exist. Most of us as Christians could not handle it anyway. Billy Graham has approached this kind of fame as an evangelist and has to live in a gated community at the top of a mountain in North Carolina and yet even Reverend Graham has not raised the dead, made the lame to walk or gave sight to the blind. I am not sure his present security would be enough if God had given him this kind of power or gift.

Some day soon I hope to see John and the other eleven all together as Jesus told them; "You will sit on 12 thrones, judging the twelve tribes of Israel." Of course Jesus was speaking of the 1000-year millennium reign which will begin exactly 7 years after an event known in the scriptures as the Blessed Hope or the Rapture. John tells us why he wrote the books that are in the Bible in his letter called 1st John:

"I write these things to you who believe in the name of the Son of God so that you may know that you have eternal life." This is the reason that John wrote the Gospel of John, three letters and the Apocalypse or The Revelation of John.

John also said in the conclusion of his Gospel: "Jesus did many other things as well. If every one of them were written down, I suppose that even the whole world would not have room for the books that would be written." If you Follow Jesus like John, then you will do things for Jesus, in fact, Jesus will do these things through you. This is why the things that Jesus did could not be written in books, because everything we do is really Jesus doing it through us. How many millions will be in heaven some day due to the writings, teachings and ministry of the Last of the Apostles?

Have you ever used the verse John 3:16? John wrote this too because he wanted everyone who read his book to follow Jesus. I hope you are following Jesus just like John did. John believed that age did make a difference because Jesus said that you must become like a little Child, to enter the Kingdom of Heaven. Jesus called John the one whom He loved!" After following his sandals in the dust, I love him too!

Sandals in the Dust

Epilogue

In the last twelve chapters we have covered the social and historical backgrounds of some of the most influential people of all time. Let us contrast them with others who have brought about great change. The biggest changes in world history were always brought about either by divine or human violence of some kind.

The flood was an act of an angry and just God who was punishing the world for their sin. This was an act of supernatural violence. The first sin in the Garden of Eden was an act of betrayal almost akin to child abuse, Adam and Eve as innocent as children were led to death and mortality by Satan in his jealous desire to control the Earth.

All the major kingdoms were spawned not through acts of love and assurance and faith, but through acts of violence, war and conquest. From the Egyptians to the Babylonians of old and on into our own century, it is through acts of violence that we achieve. The amount of violence done today and throughout the centuries in the name of furthering or purifying the true faith is rather depressing or just an insight to what kind of men we really are.

In contrast, unlike any other movement of faith since the beginning of time, Christianity spread on the foundation of "Love your Enemies and pray for them that despitefully use you." Twelve men in the space of 6 decades covered the entire known world with the Gospel. Christian Churches were visible from the borders of China all the way to the shores of England; from the north of Russia all the way to the far reaches of Africa.

The written word took shape and a whole New Testament of Jesus Christ was copied and presented in several different languages. This movement cannot be compared with the Islamic movement which even to this day relies on violence and death to promote its growth. There can be only one answer as to why these twelve ordinary men were so successful: They were inspired, led and guided by the one true God and the Holy Spirit which for the first time, dwelt in man, not just upon him. These men lived up to the words of Jesus when he told them that they would "do greater things"

These were the Sandals in the Dust that changed the whole world. These are the men that we as Americans owe our God Given freedom and faith. If you have a home in Heaven today, you owe it to the men and women who walked the dusty trail that leads us to Heaven. Our Churches, our Bible, our traditions and our doctrine of worship are all due to the work of these simple men. We have all heard of the footprints in the sand, but I say that these men made tracks in the dust and we can follow them. Jesus said that we must work while there is still light. The light is now fading and the night is coming, but hopefully I have shed a little light on the trail of these Men who walked so long ago.

Footprints fade quickly in the Dust; we must follow while there is still light!

1117460

Made in the USA